LITTLE LENIN LIBRARY
VOLUME 4

WHAT IS TO BE DONE?

BY V·I·LENIN

INTERNATIONAL PUBLISHERS
381 FOURTH AVENUE · NEW YORK 16

WHAT IS TO BE DONE?

Burning Questions of Our Movement

> . . . Party struggles . . . give a
> party strength and life. . . . The best
> proof of the weakness of a party is
> its diffuseness and its blurring of
> clear-cut differences. . . . A party be-
> comes stronger by purging itself.
>
> [From a letter by Lassalle to Marx,
> dated June 24, 1852.]

WHAT IS TO BE DONE?

Burning Questions of Our Movement

BY

V. I. LENIN

INTERNATIONAL PUBLISHERS
NEW YORK

HX314
L342
1929

CONTENTS

EDITOR'S FOREWORD

What Is To Be Done? is one of Lenin's outstanding revolutionary writings. It has long been a classic in its field. The first generation of Russian Bolsheviks, which includes many of the present Soviet leaders, have been brought up on this brilliant exposition of the policies and tactics of the revolutionary Socialist movement. Its uniqueness in Russian Marxist literature is due to the way it treats the rôle of the Party in the revolutionary struggle—a subject to which slight attention was paid up to that time. The subtitle, "Burning Questions of Our Movement," which Lenin gave to this brochure, indicates how deeply he felt the need of calling attention to the problem of organisation.

What were these "burning questions" which Lenin, soon after his return from Siberian exile, posed and to which he gave answers, first in articles in the *Iskra* ("The Urgent Tasks of Our Movement," December, 1900; "Where To Begin," May, 1901)* and finally developed in *What Is To Be Done?*, published in March, 1902?

Ideologically, Marxism had won a decisive victory over Populism which exercised hegemony among advanced Russian society and revolutionary intelligentsia during the seventies and eighties. In his early writings Lenin himself carried on sharp polemics against Populist and other utopian perversions of Socialism, thereby greatly contributing to the Marxist literary campaign designed to check their influence on the nascent revolutionary workers' movement.

The Marxist movement at that time suffered, however, from two basic weaknesses. The first was the tendency prevalent in a section of the movement and characterised as Economism, which maintained that the economic struggles of the workers for the improvement of their immediate working and living conditions should be the chief preoccupation of the labor movement. The struggle against tsarism, the Economists proposed to leave to the liberal bourgeoisie to whom they ascribed a monopoly in that field. Lenin and other revolutionary Socialists could not but consider such a policy as a travesty on Marxism, as a complete break with the nature and aims of the revolutionary labor movement, the very essence of which, they held,

---

* V. I. Lenin, *The Iskra Period*, Book I, pp. 53-58; 109-116.

was the struggle for power. Lenin goes hammer and tongs after all those who attempt to separate the struggle against the tsarist government from that against the capitalists, and brands the pure and simple trade unionism of the Economists as thoroughly reactionary and inimical to the interests of the workers.

The second weakness which Lenin vigorously attacks in this study is the question of organisation. He raises this problem to the political importance it deserves and makes an impassioned appeal to scrap the existing form of organisation and build a theoretically sound party, revolutionary in purpose and national in scope. Although formally organised into a party a few years before (1898), the Marxist movement consisted of little more than small circles, each carrying on a more or less independent existence and engaging in sporadic and planless activities. This loose aggregation of revolutionists, carrying on their work in primitive, handicraft fashion, and depending on the spontaneity of the masses, could not, according to Lenin, become the organiser and leader of the revolutionary struggles which were rapidly developing and which were involving larger and larger masses of workers. Only a centralised party, working according to a carefully prepared plan, with each member assigned a specific task for which he is to be held accountable, could successfully lead the Russian workingclass in the struggle against capitalist exploitation and tsarist rule.

"If we have a strongly organised party, a single strike may grow into a political demonstration, into a political victory over the government," Lenin wrote sometime before he began to work on *What Is To Be Done?* Obviously, the party as he conceived it, had to consist of members "who shall devote to the revolution not only their spare evenings, but the whole of their lives."

Written thirty years ago, *What Is To Be Done?* still retains its freshness because of the revolutionary enthusiasm which permeates its pages and the great lessons it has today for the workers in capitalist countries who would build their revolutionary parties after the pattern fashioned by Lenin during the formative period of the Bolshevik Party.

ALEXANDER TRACHTENBERG.

December, 1931.

WHAT IS TO BE DONE?

PREFACE

ACCORDING to the author's original plan, the present pamphlet was intended for the purpose of developing in greater detail the ideas that were expressed in the article he wrote in *Iskra*, No. 4, May, 1901, entitled "Where to Begin." * First of all, we must apologise to the reader for this belated fulfilment of the promise made in that article (and repeated in reply to many private enquiries and letters). One of the reasons for this belatedness was the attempt to combine all the Social-Democratic organisations abroad which was undertaken in June last (1901). Naturally, one wanted to see the results of this attempt, for had it been successful, it would perhaps have been necessary to express *Iskra's* views on organisation from another point of view. In any case, such success promised to put an end very quickly to the existence of two separate tendencies in Russian Social-Democracy. As the reader knows, the attempt failed, and, as we shall try to show farther on, failure was inevitable after the new turn *Rabocheye Dyelo* took in its issue No. 10 towards Economism. It was found to be absolutely necessary to commence a determined fight against these diffused, ill-defined, but very persistent tendencies, which may degenerate into many diverse forms. Accordingly, the original plan of the pamphlet was changed and considerably enlarged.

Its main theme was to have been the three questions presented in the article: "Where to Begin," *viz.*, the character and the principal content of our political agitation; our organisational tasks; and the plan for setting up simultaneously in various parts of the country, a militant, All-Russian organisation. These questions have long engaged the mind of the author, and he tried to raise them in the *Rabocheye Gazeta* at the time one of the unsuccessful attempts was made to revive that paper (*cf.* Chap. V). But the original plan to confine this pamphlet to these three questions, and to express our views as far as possible in a positive form without, or almost without, entering into polemics, proved quite impracticable for two

* See V. I. Lenin, *The Iskra Period*, Book I, p. 109.—*Ed.*

reasons. One was that Economism proved to be more virile than we supposed (we employ the term Economism in the broad sense as it was explained in *Iskra* No. 12, December, 1901, in an article entitled "A Conversation with Defenders of Economism," which represented a synopsis, as it were, of the present pamphlet).* It became unquestionably clear that the differences regarding the solution of the three problems mentioned were to be explained to a much greater degree by the fundamental antagonism between the two tendencies in Russian Social-Democracy than by differences over practical questions. The second reason was that the astonishment displayed by the Economists concerning the views we expressed in *Iskra* revealed quite clearly that we often speak in different tongues, and therefore *cannot* come to any understanding without going over the whole range of questions *ab ovo*; ** that it was necessary to attempt in the simplest possible style, illustrated by numerous and concrete examples, *systematically "to clear up" all* the fundamental points of difference with *all* the Economists. I resolved to make this attempt to "clear up" these points, fully realising that it would greatly increase the size of the pamphlet and delay its publication, but I saw *no other way* of fulfilling the promise I made in the article "Where to Begin." In apologising for the belated publication of the pamphlet I also have to apologise for its numerous literary shortcomings. I had to work *under great pressure*, and frequently had to interrupt the writing of it for other work.

The three questions mentioned before still represent the main theme of this pamphlet, but I had to start out with the examination of two other, more general questions, *viz.*, Why does an "innocent" and "natural" slogan like "freedom of criticism" represent a fighting watchword for us at the present time? And why can we not agree on even so important a question as the rôle of Social-Democracy in relation to the spontaneous mass movement? Furthermore, the exposition of our views on the character and the content of political agitation developed into an explanation of the difference between trade-union politics and Social-Democratic politics, and the exposition of our views on organisational tasks developed into an explanation of the difference between primitive methods, which satisfy the Economists, and an organisation of revolutionists, which **in our**

* See *The Iskra Period*, Book II, p. 65.—*Ed.*
** Literally "from the egg"; from the beginning.—*Ed.*

10

opinion is essential. Moreover, I insist more strongly than ever on the plan for a national political newspaper, the more so because of the weakness of the arguments that were levelled against it, and because the question that I put in the article "Where to Begin" as to how we can set to work simultaneously, all over the country, to establish the organisation we require was never really answered. Finally, in the concluding part of this pamphlet I hope to prove that we did all we could to avoid a rupture with the Economists, but the rupture proved inevitable; that *Rabocheye Dyelo* acquired special, "historical," if you will, significance not so much because it expressed consistent Economism, but because it fully and strikingly expressed the confusion and vacillation that mark a *whole period* in the history of Russian Social-Democracy, and that therefore, the polemics with *Rabocheye Dyelo*, which at first sight may seem excessively detailed, also acquires significance; for we can make no progress until we have completely liquidated this period.

February, 1902.

I

DOGMATISM AND "FREEDOM OF CRITICISM"

A. What is "Freedom of Criticism"?

"Freedom of criticism," this undoubtedly is the most fashionable slogan at the present time, and the one most frequently employed in the controversies between the Socialists and democrats of all countries. At first sight, nothing would appear to be more strange than the solemn appeals by one of the parties to the dispute for freedom of criticism. Can it be that some of the progressive parties have raised their voices against the constitutional law of the majority of European countries which guarantees freedom to science and scientific investigation? "Something must be wrong here," an onlooker who has not yet fully appreciated the nature of the disagreements among the controversialists will say, when he hears this fashionable slogan repeated at every cross-road. "Evidently this slogan is one of the conventional phrases which, like a nickname, becomes legitimatised by custom," he will conclude.

In fact, it is no secret that two separate tendencies have been formed in international Social-Democracy.* The fight between these tendencies now flares up in a bright flame, and now dies down and smoulders under the ashes of imposing "resolutions for an armistice." What this "new" tendency, which adopts a "critical" attitude

---

* This, perhaps, is the first occasion in the history of modern Socialism that controversies between various tendencies within the Socialist movement have grown from national into international controversies; and this is extremely encouraging. Formerly, the disputes between the Lassalleans and the Eisenachers, between the Guesdists and the Possibilists, between the Fabians and the Social-Democrats, and beween the Narodniki and the Social-Democrats in Russia, remained purely national disputes, reflected purely national features and proceeded, as it were, on different planes. At the present time (this is quite evident now) the English Fabians, the French Ministerialists, the German Bernsteinists [revisionists.—*Ed.*], and the Russian "Critics"— all belong to the same family, all extol each other, learn from each other, and are rallying their forces against "doctrinaire" Marxism. Perhaps, in this first real battle with Socialist opportunism, international revolutionary Social-Democracy will become sufficiently hardened to be able, at last, to put an end to the political reaction, long reigning in Europe.

towards "obsolete doctrinaire" Marxism represents, has been *stated* with sufficient precision by Bernstein, and *demonstrated* by Millerand.

Social-Democracy must change from a party of the social revolution into a democratic party of social reforms. Bernstein has surrounded this political demand by a whole battery of symmetrically arranged "new" arguments and reasonings. The possibility of putting Socialism on a scientific basis and of proving that it is necessary and inevitable from the point of view of the materialist conception of history was denied; the fact of increasing poverty, proletarianisation, the growing acuteness of capitalist contradictions, were also denied. The very conception of *"ultimate aim"* was declared to be unsound, and the idea of the dictatorship of the proletariat was absolutely rejected. It was denied that there is any difference in principle between liberalism and Socialism. *The theory of the class struggle* was rejected on the grounds that it could not be applied to strictly democratic society, governed according to the will of the majority, etc.

Thus, the demand for a decided change from revolutionary Social-Democracy to bourgeois reformism, was accompanied by a no less decided turn towards bourgeois criticism of all the fundamental ideas of Marxism. As this criticism of Marxism has been going on for a long time now, from the political platform, from university chairs, in numerous pamphlets, and in a number of scientific works, as the younger generation of the educational classes have been systematically trained for decades on this criticism, it is not surprising that the "new, critical" tendency in Social-Democracy should spring up, all complete, like Minerva from the head of Jupiter. This new tendency did not have to grow and develop, it was transferred bodily from bourgeois literature to Socialist literature.

If Bernstein's theoretical criticism and political yearnings are still obscure to any one, the trouble the French have taken to demonstrate the "new method" should remove all ambiguities. In this instance, also, France has justified its old reputation as the country in which "more than anywhere else the historical class struggles were always fought to a finish" [Engels, in his introduction to Marx's *Eighteenth Brumaire*]. The French Socialists have commenced, not to theorise, but to act. The more developed democratic political conditions in France have permitted them to put Bernsteinism into practice immediately, with its inevitable consequences. Millerand has provided an excellent example of practical Bernstein-ism. It is not surprising that he so zealously defends and praises Bernstein and Volmar! Indeed, if Social-Democracy, in essentials, is merely a reformist party, and must be bold enough to admit this openly, then, not only has a Socialist the right to join a bour-geois cabinet, but he ought always to strive to obtain places in it. If democracy, in essence, means the abolition of class domination, then why should not a Socialist minister charm the whole bourgeois world by orations on class co-operation? Why should he not remain in the cabinet even after the shooting down of workers by gendarmes has exposed, for the hundredth and thousandth time, the real nature of the democratic co-operation of classes? Why should he not personally take part in welcoming the Tsar, for whom the French Socialists now have no other sobriquet than "Hero of the Gallows, Knout and Banishment" (*knouteur, pendeur et deporta-teur*)? And the reward for this humiliation and self-degradation of Socialism in the face of the whole world, for the corruption of the Socialist consciousness of the working class—the only thing that can guarantee victory—the reward for this is, imposing *plans* for niggardly reforms, so niggardly in fact, that much more has been obtained even from bourgeois governments.

He who does not deliberately close his eyes cannot fail to see that the new "critical" tendency in Socialism is nothing more nor less than a new species of *opportunism*. And if we judge people not by the brilliant uniforms they deck themselves in, not by the im-posing appellations they give themselves, but by their actions, and by what they actually advocate, it will be clear that "freedom of criticism" means freedom for an opportunistic tendency in Social-Democracy, the freedom to convert Social-Democracy into a demo-cratic reformist party, the freedom to introduce bourgeois ideas and bourgeois elements into Socialism.

"Freedom" is a grand word, but under the banner of Free Trade the most predatory wars were conducted: under the banner of "free labour," the toilers were robbed. The term "freedom of criticism" contains the same inherent falsehood. Those who are really con-vinced that they have advanced science, would demand, not freedom for the new views to continue side by side with the old, but the substitution of the old views by the new views. The cry "Long live freedom of criticism," that is heard to-day, too strongly calls to mind the fable of the empty barrel.*

We are marching in a compact group along a precipitous and difficult path, firmly holding each other by the hand. We are surrounded on all sides by enemies, and are under their almost constant fire. We have combined voluntarily, especially for the purpose of fighting the enemy and not to retreat into the adjacent marsh, the inhabitants of which, right from the very outset, have reproached us with having separated ourselves into an exclusive group, and with having chosen the path of struggle instead of the path of conciliation. And now several in our crowd begin to cry out: Let us go into this marsh! And when we begin to shame them, they retort: How conservative you are! Are you not ashamed to deny us the right to invite you to take a better road!

Oh yes, gentlemen! You are free, not only to invite us, but to go yourselves wherever you will, even into the marsh. In fact, we think that the marsh is your proper place, and we are prepared to render *you* every assistance to get there. Only, let go of our hands, don't clutch at us, and don't besmirch the grand word "freedom"; for we too are "free" to go where we please, free, not only to fight against the marsh, but also those who are turning towards the marsh.

B. THE NEW ADVOCATES OF "FREEDOM OF CRITICISM"

Now, this slogan ("Freedom of Criticism") is solemnly advanced in No. 10 of *Rabocheye Dyelo*, the organ of the League of Russian Social-Democrats Abroad, not as a theoretical postulate, but as a political demand, as a reply to the question: "Is it possible to unite the Social-Democratic organisations operating abroad?"—"In order that unity may be durable, there must be freedom of criticism" [p. 36].

From this statement two very definite conclusions must be drawn: 1. That *Rabocheye Dyelo* has taken the opportunist tendency in international Social-Democracy under its wing; and 2. That *Rabocheye Dyelo* demands freedom for opportunism in Russian Social-Democracy. We shall examine these conclusions.

Rabocheye Dyelo is "particularly" displeased with *Iskra's* and

---

* The allusion here is to Krylov's fable about the full and empty barrels rolling down the street, the second with much more noise than the first.—*Ed.*

Zarya's "inclination to predict a rupture between the *Mountain* and the *Gironde* in international Social-Democracy." *

> Generally speaking [writes Krichevsky, editor of *Rabocheye Dyelo*] this talk about the *Mountain* and the *Gironde* that is heard in the ranks of Social-Democracy, represents a shallow historical analogy, which looks strange when it comes from the pen of a Marxist. The Mountain and the Gironde did not represent two different temperaments, or intellectual tendencies, as idealist historians may think, but two different classes, or strata—the middle bourgeoisie on the one hand, and the petty bourgeoisie and the proletariat on the other. In the modern Socialist movement, however, there is no conflict of class interests; the Socialist movement in its entirety, *all* of its diverse forms [B. K.'s italics] including the most pronounced Bernsteinists stand on the basis of the class interests of the proletariat, and of the proletarian class struggle for political and economic emancipation [pp. 32-33].

A bold assertion! B. Krichevsky, have you heard the fact long ago noted, that it is precisely the extensive participation of the "academic" *stratum* in the Socialist movement in recent years that has secured the rapid spread of Bernsteinism? And what is most important—on what does our author base his opinion that even "the most pronounced Bernsteinists" stand on the basis of the class struggle for the political and economic emancipation of the proletariat? No one knows. This determined defence of the most pronounced Bernsteinists is not supported by any kind of argument whatever. Apparently, the author believes that if he repeats what the pronounced Bernsteinists say about themselves, his assertion requires no proof. But can anything more "shallow" be imagined than an opinion of a whole tendency that is based on nothing more than what the representatives of that tendency say about themselves? Can anything more shallow be imagined than the subsequent "homily" about the two different, and even diametrically opposite, types, or paths, of party development? [*Rabocheye Dyelo*, pp. 33-35.] The German Social-Democrats, you see, recognise complete freedom of criticism, but the French do not, and it is precisely the latter that present an example of the "harmfulness of intolerance."

* A comparison between the two tendencies in the revolutionary proletariat (the revolutionary and the opportunist), and the two tendencies among the revolutionary bourgeoisie in the eighteenth century (the Jacobin Mountain and the Gironde) was made in a leading article in *Iskra*, No. 2, February, 1901, written by Plekhanov. The Cadets, the *Bezzaglavtsi* and the Mensheviks to this day love to refer to the Jacobinism in Russian Social-Democracy but they prefer to remain silent about or . . . to forget the circumstances in which Plekhanov used this term for the first time against the Right Wing of Social-Democracy. [Lenin's note to 1908 edition.—*Ed.*]

To which we reply that the very example B. Krichevsky quotes, illustrates how even those who regard history, literally from the Ilovaisky * point-of-view sometimes describe themselves as Marxists. Of course, there is no need whatever, in explaining the unity of the German Socialist Party and the dismembered state of the French Socialist Party, to search for the special features in the history of the respective countries, to compare the conditions of military semi-absolutism in the one country with republican parliamentarism in the other, or to analyse the effects of the Paris Commune and the effects of the anti-Socialist laws in Germany; to compare the economic life and economic development of the two countries, or recall that "the unexampled growth of German Social-Democracy" was accomplished by a strenuous struggle unexampled in the history of Socialism, not only against the theoreticians (Muehlberger, Duehring),** the Socialists of the Chair, but also against mistaken tactics (Lassalle), etc., etc. All that is superfluous! The French quarrel among themselves because they are intolerant; the Germans are united because they are good fellows.

And observe, this piece of matchless profundity is intended to "refute" the fact which is a complete answer to the defence of Bernsteinism. The question as to whether the Bernsteinists stand on the basis of the class struggle of the proletariat can be completely and irrevocably answered only by historical experience. Consequently, the example of France is the most important one in this respect, because France is the only country in which the Bernsteinists attempted to stand independently on their own feet with the warm approval of their German colleagues (and partly also of the

* Ilovaisky—the writer of official school text books on history noted for his reactionary treatment of Russian history.—*Ed.*

** At the time Engels hurled his attack against Duehring, many representatives of German Social-Democracy inclined towards the latter's views, and accusations of acerbity, intolerance, uncomradely polemics, etc., were publicly hurled at Engels at the party congress. At the congress of 1877, Johann Most, supported by his comrades, moved a resolution to prohibit the publication of Engels' articles in the *Vorwaerts* because "they did not represent the interests of the overwhelming majority of the readers," and Vahlteich declared that the publication of these articles had caused great damage to the party, that Duehring had also rendered services to Social-Democracy: 'We must utilise the services of all those who offer them in the interest of the party; let the professors engage in polemics if they care to do so, but the *Vorwaerts* is not the place to conduct them in" [*Vorwaerts*, No. 65, June 6, 1877]. Here we have another example of the defence of "freedom of criticism," and it would do our legal critics and illegal opportunists who love so much to quote examples from the Germans, a deal of good to ponder over it!

Russian opportunists). [*Cf. Rabocheye Dyelo*, Nos. 2-3, pp. 83-84]. The reference to the "intolerance" of the French, apart from its "historical" significance (in the Nozdrev sense),* turns out to be merely an attempt to obscure a very unpleasant fact with angry invectives.

But we are not even prepared to make a present of the Germans to B. Krichevsky and to the other numerous champions of "freedom of criticism." The "most pronounced Bernsteinists" are still tolerated in the ranks of the German Party only because they *submit* to the Hanover resolution which emphatically rejected Bernstein's "amendments," and to the Luebeck resolution, which, notwithstanding the diplomatic terms in which it is couched, contains a direct warning to Bernstein. It is a debatable point from the standpoint of the interests of the German party, as to whether diplomacy was appropriate in this case and whether, in this case, a bad peace is better than a good quarrel.** Opinions may differ in regard to the expediency or not of the *methods* employed to reject Bernsteinism, but the fact remains that the German party *did* reject Bernsteinism on two occasions. Therefore, to think that the German example endorses the thesis: "The most pronounced Bernsteinists stand for the proletarian class struggle, for its economic and political emancipation," means to fail absolutely to understand what is going on before one's eyes.***

* A character in Gogol's novel *Dead Souls*. An unusual liar, rogue, and intriguer, he was frequently beaten for cheating, but he never took matters to heart; to blackmail even a friend was an ordinary thing for him and he "bore no grudge against that person."—*Ed.*

** This is a Russian proverb.—*Ed.*

*** It must be observed that *Rabocheye Dyelo* always confines itself to a bare statement of facts concerning Bernsteinism, and "refrains" from expressing its own opinion on it. See, for example, the reports of the Stuttgart Congress in Nos. 2-3 [p. 66], in which all the disagreements are reduced to disagreements over "tactics," and the bare statement is made that the overwhelming majority remain true to the previous revolutionary tactics. Or take Nos. 4-5 [p. 25 *ff.*], in which we have a bare paraphrasing of the speeches delivered at the Hanover Congress, and a reprint of the resolution moved by Bebel. An explanation and criticism of Bernstein is again put off (as was the case in Nos. 2-3) to be dealt with in a "special article." Curiously enough, in Nos. 4-5 [p. 33], we read the following: ". . . the views expounded by Bebel have the support of the enormous majority of the congress," and a few lines lower: ". . . David defended Bernstein's views. . . . First of all, he tried to show that . . . Bernstein and his friends, after all is said and done [*sic!*], stand for class struggle. . . ." This was written in December, 1899, and in September, 1901, *Rabocheye Dyelo*, having perhaps lost faith in the correctness of Bebel's views, repeats David's views as its own!

More than that. As we have already observed, *Rabocheye Dyelo* comes before *Russian* Social-Democracy, demands "freedom of criticism," and defends Bernsteinism. Apparently, it came to the conclusion that we were unfair to our "critics" and Bernsteinists. To whom were we unfair, when and how? About this not a word. *Rabocheye Dyelo* does not name a single Russian critic or Bernsteinist! All that is left for us to do is to make one of two possible suppositions: First, that the unfairly treated party is none other than *Rabocheye Dyelo* itself (and that appears to be confirmed by the fact that in the two articles in No. 10 reference is made only to the insults hurled at the *Rabocheye Dyelo* by *Zarya* and *Iskra*). If that is the case, how is the strange fact to be explained that *Rabocheye Dyelo,* which always vehemently dissociates itself from Bernsteinism, could not defend itself, without putting in a word on behalf of the "most pronounced Bernsteinists" and of freedom of criticism? The second supposition is, that a third party has been treated unfairly. If the second supposition is correct, why should not this party be named?

We see, therefore, that *Rabocheye Dyelo* is continuing to play the game of hide and seek that it has played (as we shall prove below) ever since it commenced publication. And note the *first* practical application of this much-extolled "freedom of criticism." As a matter of fact, not only has it now been reduced to abstention from all criticism, but also to abstention from expressing independent views altogether. The very *Rabocheye Dyelo,* which avoids mentioning Russian Bernsteinism as if it were a shameful disease (to use Starover's apt expression) proposes, for the treatment of this disease, *to copy word for word* the latest German prescription for the treatment of the German variety of the disease! Instead of freedom of criticism—slavish (worse: monkey-like) imitation! The very same social and political content of modern international opportunism reveals itself in a variety of ways according to its national characteristics. In one country the opportunists long ago came out under a separate flag, while in others, they ignore theory, and conduct a Radical-Socialist policy of practical politics. In a third country, several members of the revolutionary party have deserted to the camp of opportunism and strive to achieve their aims not by an open struggle for principles and for new tactics, but by gradual, unobserved, and, if one may so express it, unpunishable corruption of their party. In a fourth country again, similar deserters employ the same methods in the twilight of their political slavishness, and with an extremely original combination of "legal" with "illegal" activity, etc., etc. To talk about freedom of criticism and Bernsteinism as a condition for uniting the *Russian* Social-Democrats, and not to explain how *Russian* Bernsteinism has manifested itself, and what fruits it has borne, means to talk for the purpose of saying nothing.

We shall try, if only in a few words, to say what *Rabocheye Dyelo* did not want to say (or perhaps did not even understand).

C. Criticism in Russia

The peculiar position of Russia in regard to the point we are examining is that *right from the very beginning* of the spontaneous labour movement on the one hand, and the change of progressive public opinion towards Marxism on the other, a combination was observed of obviously heterogeneous elements under a common flag for the purpose of fighting the common enemy (obsolete social and political views). We refer to the heyday of "legal Marxism." Speaking generally, this was an extremely curious phenomenon, that no one in the eighties, or the beginning of the nineties, would have believed possible. Suddenly, in a country ruled by an autocracy, in which the press is completely shackled, and in a period of intense political reaction in which even the tiniest outgrowth of political discontent and protest was suppressed, a *censored* literature springs up, advocating the theory of revolutionary Marxism, in a language extremely obscure, but understood by those "interested." The government had accustomed itself to regard only the theory of (revolutionary) Populism as dangerous without observing its internal evolution as is usually the case, and rejoicing at the criticism, levelled against it *no matter from what side it came*. Quite a considerable time elapsed (according to our Russian calculations) before the government realised what had happened and the unwieldly army of censors and gendarmes discovered the new enemy and flung itself upon him. Meanwhile, Marxian books were published one after another, Marxian journals and newspapers were published, nearly every one became a Marxist, Marxism was flattered, the Marxists were courted and the book publishers rejoiced at the extraordinary ready sale of Marxian literature. It is quite reasonable to suppose that among the Marxian novices who were carried away by

20

this stream, there was more than one "author who got a swelled head. . . ."

We can now speak calmly of this period as of an event of the past. It is no secret that the brief appearance of Marxism on the surface of our literature was called forth by the alliance between people of extreme and of extremely moderate views. In point of fact, the latter were bourgeois democrats; and this was the conclusion (so strikingly confirmed by their subsequent "critical" development), that intruded itself on the minds of certain persons even when the "alliance" was still intact.*

That being the case, does not the responsibility for the subsequent "confusion" rest mainly upon the revolutionary Social-Democrats who entered into alliance with these future "critics"? This question, together with a reply in the affirmative, is sometimes heard from people with excessively rigid views. But these people are absolutely wrong. Only those who have no reliance in themselves can fear to enter into temporary alliances with unreliable people. Besides, not a single political party could exist without entering into such alliances. The combination with the legal Marxists was in its way the first really political alliance contracted by Russian Social-Democrats. Thanks to this alliance an astonishingly rapid victory was obtained over Populism, and Marxian ideas (even though in a vulgarised form) became very widespread. Moreover, the alliance was not concluded altogether without "conditions." The proof: The burning by the censor, in 1895, of the Marxian symposium, *Materials on the Problem of the Economic Development of Russia.* If the literary agreement with the legal Marxists can be compared with a political alliance, then that book can be compared with a political treaty.

The rupture, of course, did not occur because the "allies" proved to be bourgeois democrats. On the contrary, the representatives of the latter tendency were the natural and desirable allies of the Social-Democrats in so far as their democratic tasks that were brought to the front by the prevailing situation in Russia were concerned. But an essential condition for such an alliance must be complete liberty for Socialists to reveal to the working class that its interests are diametrically opposed to the interests of the bour-

* Reference is made here to an article by E. Tulin [Lenin] written against Struve, bearing the title "Marxism, as Reflected in Bourgeois Literature." [See V. I. Lenin, *Collected Works*, Vol. I.—*Ed.*]

geoisie. However, the Bernsteinist and "critical" tendency to which the majority of the legal Marxists turned, deprived the Socialists of this liberty and corrupted Socialist consciousness by vulgarising Marxism, by preaching the toning down of social antagonisms, by declaring the idea of the social revolution and the dictatorship of the proletariat to be absurd, by restricting the labour movement and the class struggle to narrow trade unionism and to a "practical" struggle for petty, gradual reforms. This was tantamount to the bourgeois democrat's denial of Socialism's right to independence, and consequently, of its right to existence; in practice it meant a striving to convert the nascent labour movement into a tail of the liberals.

Naturally, under such circumstances a rupture was necessary. But the "peculiar" feature of Russia manifested itself in that this rupture simply meant the closing to the Social-Democrats of access to the most popular and widespread "legal" literature. The "ex-Marxists" who took up the flag of "criticism," and who obtained almost a monopoly in the "sale" of Marxism, entrenched themselves in this literature. Catchwords like: "Against orthodoxy" and "Long live freedom of criticism" (now repeated by *Rabocheye Dyelo*) immediately became the fashion, and the fact that neither the censor nor the gendarmes could resist this fashion is apparent from the publication of *three* Russian editions of Bernstein's celebrated book (celebrated in the Herostratus sense) and from the fact that the books by Bernstein, Prokopovich and others were recommended by Zubatov [*Iskra*, No. 10]. And this tendency did not confine itself to the sphere of literature. The turn towards criticism was accompanied by the turn towards Economism that was taken by Social-Democratic practical workers.

The manner in which the contacts and mutual dependence between legal criticism and illegal Economism arose and grew, is an interesting subject in itself, and may very well be treated in a special article. It is sufficient to note here that these contacts undoubtedly existed. The notoriety deservedly acquired by the *Credo* was due precisely to the frankness with which it formulated these contacts and laid down the fundamental political tendencies of Economism, *viz.:* Let the workers carry on the economic struggle (it would be more correct to say the trade union struggle, because the latter embraces also specifically labour politics), and let the Marxist intelligentsia merge with the liberals for the political "struggle."

Thus, it turned out that trade union work "among the people" meant fulfilling the first part of this task, and legal criticism meant fulfilling the second part. This statement proved to be such an excellent weapon against Economism that, had there been no *Credo*, it would have been worth inventing.

The *Credo* was not invented, but it was published without the consent and perhaps even against the will of its authors. At all events the present writer, who was partly responsible for dragging this "programme" into the light of day,* has heard complaints and reproaches to the effect that copies of the résumé of their views which were dubbed the *Credo* were distributed and even published in the press together with the protest! We refer to this episode because it reveals a very peculiar state of mind among our Economists, *viz.:* a fear of publicity. This feature is common among the Economists, and not among the authors of the *Credo* alone. It was revealed by that most outspoken and honest advocate of Economism, *Rabochaya Mysl,* and by *Rabocheye Dyelo* (which was indignant over the publication of Economist documents in the *Vademecum*), as well as by the Kiev Committee, which two years ago refused to permit the publication of its *profession de foi* ** together with a protest that had been written against it,*** and by many other individual representatives of Economism.

This fear of criticism displayed by the advocates of freedom of criticism cannot be attributed solely to craftiness (although no doubt craftiness has something to do with: It would be unwise to expose the young and as yet puny movement to the enemies' attack!) No, the majority of the Economists quite sincerely disapprove (and by the very nature of Economism they must disapprove) of all theoretical controversies, factional disagreements, of broad political questions, of schemes for organising revolutionaries, etc. "Leave all this sort of thing to the exiles abroad!" said a fairly consistent Economist to me one day, and thereby he expressed a very

* Reference is made here to the *Protest Signed by the Seventeen* against the *Credo*. The present writer took part in drawing up this protest (the end of 1899). The protest and the *Credo* were published abroad in the spring of 1900. [See V. I. Lenin, *Collected Works*, Vol. II.—*Ed.*] It is now known from the article written by Madame Kuskova, I think in *Byloye* [*Past*] that she was the author of the *Credo*, and that Mr. Prokopovich was very prominent among the Economists abroad at that time.

** Profession of faith.—*Ed.*

*** As far as we know the composition of the Kiev Committee has been changed since then.

widespread (purely trade unionist) view: Our business, he said, is the labour movement, the labour organisations, here, in our localities; all the rest are merely the inventions of doctrinaires, an "exaggeration of the importance of ideology," as the authors of the letter, published in *Iskra*, No. 12, expressed it in unison with *Rabocheye Dyelo*, No. 10.

The question now arises: Seeing what the peculiar features of Russian "criticism" and Russian Bernsteinism were, what should those who desired, in deeds and not merely in words, to oppose opportunism have done? First of all, they should have made efforts to resume the theoretical work that was only just commenced in the period of legal Marxism, and that has now again fallen on the shoulders of the illegal workers. Unless such work is undertaken the successful growth of the movement is impossible. Secondly, they should have actively combated legal "criticism" that was corrupting people's minds. Thirdly, they should have actively counteracted the confusion and vacillation prevailing in practical work, and should have exposed and repudiated every conscious or unconscious attempt to degrade our programme and tactics.

That *Rabocheye Dyelo* did none of these things is a well-known fact, and further on, we shall deal with this well-known fact from various aspects. At the moment, however, we desire merely to show what a glaring contradiction there is between the demand for "freedom of criticism" and the peculiar features of our native criticism and Russian Economism. Indeed, glance at the text of the resolution by which the League of Russian Social-Democrats Abroad endorsed the point-of-view of *Rabocheye Dyelo*.

In the interests of the further ideological development of Social-Democracy, we recognise the freedom to criticise Social-Democratic theory in party literature to be absolutely necessary in so far as this critcism does not run counter to the class and revolutionary character of this theory [*Two Congresses*, p. 10].

And what is the argument behind this resolution? The resolution "in its first part coincides with the resolution of the Luebeck Party Congress on Bernstein. . . ." In the simplicity of their souls the Leaguers failed to observe the *testimonium paupertatis* (certificate of mental poverty) they give themselves by this piece of imitativeness! . . . "But . . . in its second part, it restricts freedom of criticism much more than did the Luebeck Party Congress."

So the League's resolution was directed against the **Russian**

Bernsteinism? If it was not, then the reference to Luebeck is utterly absurd! But it is not true to say that it "restricts freedom of criticism." In passing their Hanover resolution, the Germans, point by point, rejected precisely *the amendments* proposed by Bernstein, while in their Luebeck resolution they cautioned *Bernstein personally*, and named him in the resolution. Our "free" imitators, however, *do not make a single reference to a single manifestation* of Russian "criticism" and Russian Economism, and in view of this omission, the bare reference to the class and revolutionary character of the theory, leaves exceedingly wide scope for misinterpretation, particularly when the League refuses to identify "so-called Economism" with opportunism [*Two Congresses,* p. 8]. But all this *en passant.* The important thing to note is that the opportunist attitude towards revolutionary Social-Democrats in Russia is the very opposite to that in Germany. In Germany, as we know, revolutionary Social-Democrats are in favour of preserving what is: They stand in favour of the old programme and tactics which are universally known, and after many decades of experience have become clear in all their details. The "critics" desire to introduce changes, and as these critics represent an insignificant minority, and as they are very shy and halting in their revisionist efforts, one can understand the motives of the majority in confining themselves to the dry rejection of "innovations." In Russia, however, it is the critics and Economists who are in favour of preserving what is: The "critics" wish us to continue to regard them as Marxists, and to guarantee them the "freedom of criticism" which they enjoyed to the full (for as a matter of fact they never recognised any kind of *party* ties *

* The absence of recognised party ties and party traditions by itself marks such a cardinal difference between Russia and Germany that it should have warned all sensible Socialists from being blindly imitative. But here is an example of the lengths to which "freedom of criticism" goes in Russia. Mr. Bulgakov, the Russian critic, utters the following reprimand to the Austrian critic, Hertz: "Notwithstanding the independence of his conclusions, Hertz, on this point [on co-operative societies] apparently remains tied by the opinions of his party, and although he disagrees with it in details, he dare not reject common principles" [*Capitalism and Agriculture,* Vol. II, p. 287]. The subject of a politically enslaved state, in which nine hundred and ninety-nine out of a thousand of the population are corrupted to the marrow of their bones by political subservience and completely lack the conception of party honour and party ties, superciliously reprimands a citizen of a constitutional state for being excessively "tied by the opinion of his party"! Our illegal organisations have nothing else to do, of course, but draw up resolutions about freedom of criticism. . . .

and, moreover, we never had a generally recognised party organ which could "restrict" freedom of criticism even by friendly advice); the Economists want the revolutionaries to recognise "complete equality in the movement" [*Rabocheye Dyelo* No. 10, p. 25], *i. e.*, to recognise the "legitimacy" of what exists; they do not want the "ideologists" to try to "divert" the movement from the path that "is determined by the interaction of material elements and material environment" [Letter published in *Iskra*, No. 12]; they want recognition "for the only struggle that the workers can conduct under present conditions," which in their opinion is the struggle "which they are actually conducting at the present time" [Special Supplement to *Rabochaya Mysl*, p. 14]. We Revolutionary Social-Democrats, on the contrary, are dissatisfied with this submission to elemental forces, *i. e.*, bowing to what is "at the present time"; we demand that the tactics that have prevailed in recent years be changed; we declare that "before we can unite, and in order that we may unite, we must first of all firmly and definitely draw the lines of demarcation between the various groups." (*See* announcement of the publication of *Iskra*.) * In a word, the Germans stand for what is and reject the changes; we demand changes, and reject subservience to, and conciliation with, what is.

This "little" difference our "free" copyists of German resolutions failed to notice!

D. Engels on the Importance of the Theoretical Struggle

"Dogmatism, doctrinairism," "ossification of the party—the inevitable retribution that follows the violent strait-lacing of thought," these are the enemies against which the kindly champions of "freedom of criticism" are allying their forces in *Rabocheye Dyelo*. We are very glad that this question has been brought up and we would propose only to add to it another question:

Who are to be the judges?

Before us lie two publishers' announcements. One, *The Programme of the Periodical Organ of the Russian Social-Democratic League—Rabocheye Dyelo* (Reprint from No. 1 of *Rabocheye Dyelo*), and the other, *Announcement of the Resumption of Publication of Osvobozhdeniye Truda*. Both are dated 1899, when

* See "Declaration by the Editorial Board of *Iskra*," *The Iskra Period*, Book I, p. 38.—*Ed.*

the "crisis of Marxism" had long been discussed. And what do we find? In the first production, we would seek in vain for any manifestation, or definite elucidation of the position the new organ intends to occupy. Of theoretical work and the urgent tasks that now confront it, not a word is said in this programme, nor in the supplements to it, that were passed by the Third Congress of the League in 1901 [*Two Congresses*, pp. 15-18]. During the whole of this time, the editorial board of *Rabocheye Dyelo* ignored theoretical questions, notwithstanding the fact that these questions excited the minds of Social-Democrats in all countries.

The other announcement, on the contrary, first of all points to the diminution of interest in theory observed in recent years, imperatively demands "vigilant attention to the theoretical aspect of the revolutionary movement of the proletariat," and calls for "ruthless criticism of the Bernsteinist and other anti-revolutionary tendencies in our movement. The issues of *Zarya* that have appeared show to what extent this programme was carried out.

Thus we see that high-sounding phrases against the ossification of thought, etc., conceal carelessness and helplessness in the development of theoretical ideas. The case of the Russian Social-Democrats strikingly illustrates the fact observed in the whole of Europe (and long ago observed in German Marxism) that the notorious freedom of criticism implies, not the substitution of one theory by another, but freedom from every complete and thought-out theory; it implies eclecticism and absence of principle. Those who are in the least acquainted with the actual state of our movement cannot but see that the spread of Marxism was accompanied by a certain deterioration of theoretical standards. Quite a number of people, with very little, and even totally lacking in, theoretical training, joined the movement for the sake of its practical significance and its practical successes. We can judge, therefore, how tactless *Rabocheye Dyelo* is when, with an air of invincibility, it quotes the statement of Marx that: "A single step of the real movement is worth a dozen programmes." To repeat these words in the epoch of theoretical chaos is sheer mockery. Moreover, these words of Marx are taken from his letter on the Gotha Programme, in which he *sharply condemns* eclectism in the formulation of principles: "If you must combine," Marx wrote to the party leaders, "then enter into agreements to satisfy the practical aims of the movement, but do not haggle over principles, do not make 'concessions' in theory." This was Marx's idea, and yet there are people among us who strive—in his name!—to belittle the significance of theory.

Without a revolutionary theory there can be no revolutionary movement. This cannot be insisted upon too strongly at a time when the fashionable preaching of opportunism is combined with absorption in the narrowest forms of practical activity. The importance of theory for Russian Social-Democrats is still greater for three reasons, which are often forgotten:

The first is that our party is only in the process of formation, its features are only just becoming outlined, and it has not yet completely settled its reckoning with other tendencies in revolutionary thought which threaten to divert the movement from the proper path. Indeed, in very recent times we have observed (as Axelrod long ago warned the Economists would happen) a revival of non-Social-Democratic revolutionary tendencies. Under such circumstances, what at first sight appears to be an "unimportant" mistake, may give rise to most deplorable consequences, and only the short-sighted would consider factional disputes and strict distinction of shades to be inopportune and superfluous. The fate of Russian Social-Democracy for many, many years to come may be determined by the strengthening of one or the other "shade."

The second reason is that the Social-Democratic movement is essentially an international movement. This does not mean merely that we must combat national chauvinism. It means also that a movement that is starting in a young country can be successful only on the condition that it assimilates the experience of other countries. In order to assimilate this experience, it is not sufficient merely to be acquainted with it, or simply to transcribe the latest resolutions. A critical attitude is required towards this experience, and ability to subject it to independent tests. Only those who realise how much the modern labour movement has grown in strength will understand what a reserve of theoretical forces and political (as well as revolutionary) experience is required to fulfil this task.

The third reason is that the national tasks of Russian Social-Democracy are such as have never confronted any other Socialist party in the world. Farther on we shall deal with the political and organisational duties which the task of emancipating the whole people from the yoke of autocracy imposes upon us. At the moment, we wish merely to state that the *rôle of vanguard can be fulfilled only by a party that is guided by an advanced theory.* To understand what this means concretely, let the reader call to mind the predecessors of Russian Social-Democracy like Herzen, Belinsky, Chernyshevsky and the brilliant band of revolutionists of the seventies; let him ponder over the world significance which Russian literature is now acquiring, let him . . . Oh! But that is enough!

We shall quote what Engels said in 1874 concerning the significance of theory in the Social-Democratic movement. Engels recognises *not two* forms of the great struggle Social-Democracy is conducting (political and economic), as is the fashion among us, *but three, adding to the first two also the theoretical struggle.* His recommendations to the German labour movement, which has now become practically and politically strong, are so instructive from the point of view of present-day controversies, that we hope the reader will forgive us for quoting a long passage from his Introduction to the *Peasant War in Germany*, which long ago became a literary rarity.

The German workers have two important advantages compared with the rest of Europe. First, they belong to the most theoretical people of Europe; second, they have retained that sense of theory which the so-called "educated" people of Germany have totally lost. Without German philosophy, particularly that of Hegel, German scientific Socialism (the only scientific Socialism extant) would never have come into existence. Without a sense for theory, scientific Socialism would have never become blood and tissue of the workers. What an enormous advantage this is, may be seen, on the one hand, from the indifference of the English labour movement towards all theory, which is one of the reasons why it moves so slowly, in spite of the splendid organisation of the individual unions; on the other hand, from the mischief and confusion created by Proudhonism in its original form among the Frenchmen and Belgians, and in its caricature form, as presented by Bakunin, among the Spaniards and Italians.

The second advantage is that, chronologically speaking, the Germans were the last to appear in the labour movement. In the same manner as German theoretical Socialism will never forget that it rests on the shoulders of Saint Simon, Fourier and Owen, the three who, in spite of their fantastic notions and Utopianism, belonged to the most significant heads of all time, and whose genius anticipated the correctness of which can now be proved in a scientific way, so the practical German labour movement must never forget that it has developed on the shoulders of the English and French movements, that it had utilised their experience, acquired at a heavy price, and that for this reason it was in a position to avoid their mistakes which in their time were unavoidable. Without the English trade unions and the French political workers' struggles preceding the German labour movement, without the mighty impulse given by the Paris Commune, where would we now be?

It must be said to the credit of the German workers that they utilised the advantages of their situation with rare understanding. For the first time in the history of the labour movement, the struggle is being so conducted that its three sides, the theoretical, the political, and the practical economic

29

(resistance to the capitalists), form one harmonious and well-planned entity. In this concentric attack, as it were, lies the strength and invincibility of the German movement.

It is due to this advantageous situation on the one hand, to the insular peculiarities of the British, and to the cruel oppression of the French movements on the other, that for the present moment the German workers form the vanguard of the proletarian struggle. How long events will allow them to occupy this post of honour cannot be foreseen. But as long as they are placed in it, let us hope that they will discharge their duties in the proper manner. To this end it will be necessary to double our energies in all the spheres of struggle and agitation. It is the specified duty of the leaders to gain an ever-clearer understanding of the theoretical problems, to free themselves more and more from the influence of traditional phrases inherited from the old conception of the world, and constantly to keep in mind that Socialism, having become a science, demands the same treatment as every other science —it must be studied. The task of the leaders will be to bring understanding, thus acquired and clarified, to the working masses, to spread it with increased enthusiasm, to close the ranks of the party organisations and of the labour unions with ever-greater energy. . . .

If the German workers proceed in this way they may not march exactly at the head of the movement—it is not in the interest of the movement that the workers of one country should march at the head of all—but they will occupy an honourable place on the battle line, and they will stand armed for battle when other unexpected grave trials or momentous events will demand heightened courage, heightened determination, and the will to act.*

Engels' words proved prophetic. Within a few years, the German workers were subjected to severe trials in the form of the anti-Socialist laws; but they were fully armed to meet the situation, and succeeded in emerging from it victoriously.

The Russian workers will have to undergo trials immeasurably more severe; they will have to take up the fight against a monster, compared with which anti-Socialist laws in a constitutional country are but pigmies. History has now confronted us with an immediate task which is *more revolutionary than all the immediate tasks* that confront the proletariat of any other country. The fulfilment of this task, the destruction of the most powerful bulwark, not only of European, but also (it may now be said) of Asiatic reaction, places the Russian proletariat in the vanguard of the international revolutionary proletariat. We shall have the right to count upon acquiring the honourable title already earned by our predecessors, the revolutionists of the seventies, if we succeed in inspiring our movement—which is a thousand times wider and deeper—with the same devoted determination and vigour.

* Third Edition, Leipzig, 1875. [English translation, pp. 27-30.—*Ed.*]

II

THE SPONTANEITY OF THE MASSES AND THE CLASS-CONSCIOUS-NESS OF SOCIAL-DEMOCRACY

WE have said that our movement, much wider and deeper than the movement of the seventies, must be inspired with the same devoted determination and energy that inspired the movement at that time. Indeed, no one, we think, has up till now doubted that the strength of the modern movement lies in the awakening of the masses (principally, the industrial proletariat), and that its weakness lies in the lack of consciousness and initiative among the revolutionary leaders.

However, a most astonishing discovery has been made recently, which threatens to overthrow all the views that have hitherto prevailed on this question. This discovery was made by *Rabocheye Dyelo,* which, in its controversy with *Iskra* and *Zarya,* did not confine itself to making objections on separate points, but tried to ascribe "general disagreements" to a more profound cause—to the "disagreement concerning the estimation of the *relative* importance of the spontaneous and consciously 'methodical' element." *Rabocheye Dyelo's* indictment reads: *"Belittling the importance of the objective, or spontaneous, element of development."* * To this we say: If the controversy with *Iskra* and *Zarya* resulted in absolutely nothing more than causing *Rabocheye Dyelo* to think over these "general disagreements," that single result would give us considerable satisfaction, so important is this thesis, and so clearly does it illuminate the quintessence of the present-day theoretical and political differences that exist among Russian Social-Democrats.

That is why the question of the relation between consciousness and spontaneity is of such enormous general interest, and that is why this question must be dealt with in great detail.

A. THE BEGINNING OF THE SPONTANEOUS MOVEMENT

In the previous chapter we pointed out how universally absorbed the educated youth of Russia were in the theories of Marxism in

* *Rabocheye Dyelo,* No. 10, 1901, pp. 17-18 [R. D.'s italics].

the middle of the nineties. The strikes that followed the famous St. Petersburg industrial war of 1896 also assumed a similar wholesale character. The fact that these strikes spread over the whole of Russia showed how deep the reviving popular movement was, and if we must speak of the "spontaneous element" then, of course, we must admit that this strike movement certainly bore a spontaneous character. But there is a difference between spontaneity and spontaneity. Strikes occurred in Russia in the seventies, and in the sixties (and also in the first half of the nineteenth century), and these strikes were accompanied by the "spontaneous" destruction of machinery, etc. Compared with these "revolts" the strikes of the nineties might even be described as "conscious," to such an extent do they mark the progress which the labour movement had made since that period. This shows that the "spontaneous element," in essence, represents nothing more nor less than consciousness in an *embryonic form*. Even the primitive rebellions expressed the awakening of consciousness to a certain extent: The workers abandoned their age-long faith in the permanence of the system which oppressed them. They began . . . I shall not say to understand, but to sense the necessity for collective resistance, and emphatically abandoned their slavish submission to their superiors. But all this was more in the nature of outbursts of desperation and vengeance than *struggle*. The strikes of the nineties revealed far greater flashes of consciousness: Definite demands were put forward, the time to strike was carefully chosen, known cases and examples in other places were discussed, etc. While the revolts were simply uprisings of the oppressed, the systematic strikes represented the class struggle in embryo, but only in embryo. Taken by themselves, these strikes were simply trade union struggles, but not yet Social-Democratic struggles. They testified to the awakening antagonisms between workers and employers, but the workers were not and could not be conscious of the irreconcilable antagonism of their interests to the whole of the modern political and social system, *i. e.*, it was not yet Social-Democratic consciousness. In this sense, the strikes of the nineties, in spite of the enormous progress they represented as compared with the "revolts," represented a purely spontaneous movement.

We said that *there could not yet be* Social-Democratic consciousness among the workers. This consciousness could only be brought to them from without. The history of all countries shows that the working class, exclusively by its own effort, is able to develop only trade-union consciousness, *i. e.*, it may itself realise the necessity for combining in unions, to fight against the employers and to strive to compel the government to pass necessary labour legislation, etc.*

The theory of Socialism, however, grew out of the philosophic, historical and economic theories that were elaborated by the educated representatives of the propertied classes, the intellectuals. The founders of modern scientific Socialism, Marx and Engels, themselves belonged to the bourgeois intelligentsia. Similarly, in Russia, the theoretical doctrine of Social-Democracy arose quite independently of the spontaneous growth of the labour movement; it arose as a natural and inevitable outcome of the development of ideas among the revolutionary Socialist intelligentsia. At the time of which we are speaking, *i. e.*, the middle of the nineties, this doctrine not only represented the completely formulated programme of the Emancipation of Labour group but had already won the adhesion of the majority of the revolutionary youth in Russia.

Hence, simultaneously we had both the spontaneous awakening of the masses of the workers—the awakening to conscious life and struggle, and the striving of the revolutionary youth, armed with the Social-Democratic theories, to reach the workers. In this connection it is particularly important to state the oft-forgotten (and comparatively little-known) fact that the early Social-Democrats of that period, *zealously carried on economic agitation* (being guided in this by the really useful instructions contained in the pamphlet *Agitation* that was still in manuscript) but they did not regard this as their sole task. On the contrary, *right from the very beginning* they brought up the general historical tasks of Russian Social-Democracy, and particularly the task of overthrowing the autocracy. For example, the St. Petersburg group of Social-Democrats, which was formed by the League of the Struggle for the Emancipation of the Working Class towards the end of 1895, got out the first number of the journal known as *Rabocheye Dyelo*. This number was completely ready for the press when it was seized by the gendarmes who, on the night of December 8, 1895, raided

* Trade Unionism does not exclude "politics" altogether as some imagine. Trade unions have always conducted political agitation and struggle (but not Social-Democratic ones). We shall deal with the difference between trade union politics and Social-Democratic politics in the next chapter.

the house of one of the members of the group, Anatole Alekseyevich Vaneyev,* and so the original *Rabocheye Dyelo* was not fated to see the light. The leading article in this number (which perhaps in thirty years' time some *Russkaya Starina* [*Russian Antiquary*] will discover in the archives of the Department of Police) described the historic tasks of the working class in Russia, of which the achievement of political liberty is regarded as the most important. This number also contained an article entitled, "What Are Our Cabinet Ministers Thinking Of?" which dealt with the wrecking of the premises of the elementary education committees by the police. In addition, there was some correspondence, from St. Petersburg, as well as from other parts of Russia (for example, a letter on the shooting down of the workers in the Yaroslav province). This, if we are not mistaken, "first attempt" of the Russian Social-Democrats of the nineties was not a narrow, local, and certainly not an "economic" newspaper, but one that aimed to unite the strike movement with the revolutionary movement against the autocracy, and to win all the victims of oppression and political and reactionary obscurantism over to the side of Social-Democracy. No one in the slightest degree acquainted with the state of the movement at that period could doubt that such a paper would have been fully approved of by the workers of the capital and the revolutionary intelligentsia and would have had a wide circulation. The failure of the enterprise merely showed that the Social-Democrats of that time were unable to meet the immediate requirements of the time owing to their lack of revolutionary experience and practical training. The same thing must be said with regard to the St. Petersburg *Rabochy Listok* [*Workers' Leaflet*] and particularly with regard to the *Rabochaya Gazeta* and *Manifesto* established in the spring of 1898 by the Russian Social-Democratic Labour Party. Of course, we would not dream of blaming the Social-Democrats of that time for this unpreparedness. But in order to obtain the benefit of the experience of that movement, and to learn practical lessons from it, we must thoroughly understand the causes and significance of this or that shortcoming. For that reason

* A. A. Vaneyev died in eastern Siberia in 1899, from consumption, which he contracted as a result of his solitary confinement in prison prior to his banishment. That is why we are able to publish the above information, the authenticity of which we guarantee, for it comes from persons who were closely and directly acquainted with A. A. Vaneyev.

it is extremely important to establish the fact that part (perhaps even a majority) of the Social-Democrats operating in the period of 1895-1898, quite justly considered it possible even then, at the very beginning of the "spontaneous movement," to come forward with a most extensive programme and fighting tactics.*

The lack of training of the majority of the revolutionists being quite a natural phenomenon, could not have aroused any particular fears. Since the tasks were properly defined, since the energy existed for repeated attempts to fulfil these tasks, the temporary failures were not such a great misfortune. Revolutionary experience and organisational skill are things that can be acquired provided the desire is there to acquire these qualities, provided the shortcomings are recognised—which in revolutionary activity is more than half-way towards removing them!

It was a great misfortune, however, when this consciousness began to grow dim (it was very lively among the workers of the group mentioned), when people appeared—and even Social-Democratic organs—who were prepared to regard shortcomings as virtues, who tried even to put a *theoretical* basis to *slavish cringing before spontaneity*. It is time to summarise this tendency, the substance of which is incorrectly and too narrowly described as Economism.

B. Bowing to Spontaneity
Rabochaya Mysl

Before dealing with the literary manifestation of this subservience, we would like to mention the following characteristic fact (communicated to us from the above-mentioned source), which throws

* *Iskra*, which adopts a hostile attitude towards the activities of the Social-Democrats of the end of the nineties, ignores the fact that at that time the conditions were unfavourable for any other kind of work except fighting for petty demands, declare the Economists in their Letter to Russian Social-Democratic Organs [*Iskra*, No. 12]. The facts quoted above show that the statement about "unfavourable conditions" *is diametrically opposite to the truth*. Not only at the end, but even in the middle of the nineties, all the conditions existed *for other* work, besides fighting for petty demands, all the conditions—except the sufficient training of the leaders. Instead of frankly admitting our, the ideologists', the leaders', lack of sufficient training—the Economists try to throw the blame entirely upon "the absence of conditions," upon the influence of material environment which determined the road from which it was impossible to divert the movement by any kind of ideology. What is this but slavish cringing before spontaneity, but the fact that the "ideologists" are enamoured of their own shortcomings?

some light on circumstances of the rise and growth of two diverg-
ing Russian Social-Democratic tendencies among the comrades working in St. Petersburg. In the beginning of 1897, just prior to their
banishment, A. A. Vaneyev and several of his comrades attended a
private meeting at which the "old" and "young" members of the
League of the Struggle for the Emancipation of the Working Class
were gathered. The conversation centred chiefly around the question of organisation, and particularly around the "rules for a workers' benefit club," which, in their final form, were published in
Listok Rabotnika—[*Workers' Leaflet*] Nos. 9-10, p. 46. Sharp
differences were immediately revealed between the "old" members
(the "Decembrists," as the St. Petersburg Social-Democrats jestingly
called them) and several of the "young" members (who subse-
quently took an active part in the work of *Rabochaya Mysl*), the
divergences were very great and a very heated discussion ensued.
The "young" members defended the main principles of the rules in
the form in which they were published. The "old" members said
that this was not what was wanted: That first of all it was necessary
to consolidate the League of the Struggle into an organisation of
revolutionaries which should have control of all the various workers'
benefit clubs, students' propaganda circles, etc. It goes without
saying that the controversialists had no suspicion at that time that
these disagreements were the beginning of a wide divergence; on the
contrary they regarded them as being of an isolated and casual
nature. But this fact shows that Economism did not arise and
spread in Russia without a fight on the part of the "old" Social-
Democrats (the Economists of to-day are apt to forget this). And
if this struggle has not left "documentary" traces behind it, it is
solely because the membership of the circles working at that time
underwent such constant change that no continuity was established
and, consequently, differences were not recorded in any documents.
   The appearance of *Rabochaya Mysl* brought Economism to the
light of day, but not all at once. We must picture to ourselves
concretely the conditions of the work and the short-livedness of
the majority of the Russian circles (and only those who have experienced this can have any exact idea of it), in order to understand how much there was accidental in the successes and failures
of the new tendency in various towns, and why for a long time
neither the advocates nor the opponents of this "new" tendency
could make up their minds, indeed they had no opportunity to do

so—as to whether this was really a new tendency or whether it was merely an expression of the lack of training of certain individuals. For example, the first mimeographed copies of *Rabochaya Mysl* never reached the great majority of Social-Democrats, and we are able to refer to the leading article in the first number only because it was reproduced in an article by V. I. [*Listok Rabotnika*, Nos. 9-10, p. 47*ff.*], who, of course, did not fail zealously, but unreasonably to extol the new paper, which was so different from the papers and the schemes for papers mentioned above.* And this leading article deserves to be dealt with in detail because it so strongly expresses *the spirit of Rabochaya Mysl* and Economism generally.

After referring to the fact that the arm of the "blue-coats" could never stop the progress of the labour movement, the leading article goes on to say: ". . . The virility of the labour movement is due to the fact that the workers themselves are at last taking their fate in their own hands, and out of the hands of the leaders," and this fundamental thesis is then developed in greater detail. As a matter of fact the leaders (*i. e.*, the Social-Democrats, the organisers of the League of the Struggle) were, one might say, torn out of the hands of the workers by the police; ** yet it is made to appear that the workers were fighting against the leaders and eventually liberated themselves from their yoke! Instead of calling upon the workers to go forward towards the consolidation of the revolutionary organisation, and to the expansion of political activity, they began to call for a *regress* to the purely trade-union struggle. They announced that "the economic basis of the movement is eclipsed by the effort never to forget the political idea," and that the watchword for the movement was "Fight for an economic position" (!) or to go even one better, "The workers for the workers." It was de-

* It should be stated in passing that the praise of *Rabochaya Mysl* in November, 1898, when Economism had become fully defined, especially abroad, emanated from that same V. I., who, very soon after, became one of the editors of *Rabocheye Dyelo*. And yet *Rabocheye Dyelo* denied that there were two tendencies in Russian Social-Democracy, and continues to deny it to this day.

** That this simile is a correct one is shown by the following characteristic fact. When after the arrest of the "Decembrists," the news was spread among the workers on the Schlusselburg Road that the discovery and arrest was facilitated by an agent provocateur, N. M. Mikhailov, a dental surgeon, who had been in contact with a group associated with the "Decembrists," they were so enraged that they decided to kill him.

clared that strike funds "are more valuable for the movement than 100 other organisations." (Compare this statement made in 1897 with the controversy between the "Decembrists" and the young members in the beginning of 1897.) Catch-words like: "We must concentrate, not on the 'cream' of the workers, but on the 'average' worker—the mass worker"; "Politics always obediently follows economics," * etc., etc., became the fashion, and exercised irresistible influence upon the masses of the youth who were attracted to the movement, but who, in the majority of cases, were acquainted only with legally expounded fragments of Marxism.

Consciousness was completely overwhelmed by spontaneity—the spontaneity of the "Social-Democrats" who repeated V. V.'s "ideas," the spontaneity of those workers who were carried away by the arguments that a kopeck added to a rouble was worth more than Socialism and politics, and that they must "fight, knowing that they are fighting not for some future generations, but for themselves and their children." [Leading article in *Rabochaya Mysl*, No. 1.] Phrases like these have always been the favourite weapons of the Western European bourgeoisie, who, while hating Socialism, strove (like the German "Sozial-Politiker" Hirsch) to transplant English trade unionism to their own soil, and to preach to the workers that the purely trade-union struggle is the struggle for their own and their children's welfare, and not a struggle for some kind of Socialism that will be realised only in the very remote future.** And now the "V. V.'s of Russian Social-Democracy" repeat these bourgeois phrases. It is important at this point to note three circumstances, which will be useful to us in our further analysis of *contemporary* differences.***

* These quotations are taken from the leading article, in the first number of *Rabochaya Mysl* already referred to. One can judge from this, the degree of theoretical training possessed by these "V. V.'s of Russian Social-Democracy," who kept repeating the crude vulgarisms of "economic materialism" at a time when the Marxists were carrying on a literary war against the real V. V. who had long ago been dubbed "a past master of reactionary deeds" for holding *similar* views on the relation between politics and economics!

** The Germans even have a special expression: *Nur Gewerkschaftler,* which means an advocate of the "pure and simple" trade-union struggle.

*** We emphasise the word *contemporary* for the benefit of those who may pharisaically shrug their shoulders and say: It is easy enough to attack *Rabochaya Mysl* now, but is not all this ancient history? *Mutato nomine de te fabula narratur* [Change the name and the tale refers to you.—Ed.], we reply to such contemporary pharisees whose complete mental subjection to *Rabochaya Msyl* will be *proved* farther on.

First of all, the overwhelming of consciousness by spontaneity to which we referred above, also took place *spontaneously*. This may sound like a pun, but alas, it is the bitter truth. It did not take place as a result of an open struggle between two diametrically opposed points-of-view, in which one gained the victory over the other; it occurred because an increasing number of "old" revolutionaries were "torn away" by the gendarmes, and because increasing numbers of "young" members and "V. V.'s of Russian Social-Democracy" came upon the scene. Every one, who I shall not say has participated in the *contemporary* Russian movement, but who has at least breathed its atmosphere, knows perfectly well that this was so. And the reason why we, nevertheless, strongly urge the reader to ponder well this universally known fact, and why we quote the facts, as an illustration, so to speak, about the *Rabocheye Dyelo* as it first appeared, and about the controversy between the "old" and the "young" at the beginning of 1897, is that certain persons are speculating on the public's (or the very youthful youth's) ignorance of these facts, and are boasting of their "democracy." We shall return to this point farther on.

Secondly, in the very first literary manifestation of Economism, we observe the extremely curious and highly characteristic phenomenon—from the point-of-view of the differences prevailing among contemporary Social-Democrats—that the adherents of the "pure and simple" labour movement, the worshippers of the closest "organic" (the term used by *Rabocheye Dyelo*) contacts with the proletarian struggle, the opponents of the non-labour intelligentsia (notwithstanding that it is a Socialist intelligentsia) are compelled, in order to defend their positions, to resort to the arguments of the *bourgeois* "pure and simple" trade unionists. This shows that right from the outset, *Rabochaya Mysl* began unconsciously to carry out the programme of the *Credo*. This shows (what the *Rabocheye Dyelo* cannot understand) that subservience to the spontaneity of the labour movement, the belittling of the rôle of "the conscious element," of the rôle of Social-Democracy, *means, whether one likes it or not, growth of influence of bourgeois ideology among the workers.* All those who talk about "exaggerating the importance of ideology," * about exaggerating the rôle of the conscious elements,** etc., imagine that the pure and simple labour movement

* Letter by the Economists, in *Iskra*, No. 12.
** *Rabocheye Dyelo*, No. 10.

can work out an independent ideology for itself, if only the workers "take their fate out of the hands of the leaders." But in this they are profoundly mistaken. To supplement what has been said above, we shall quote the following profoundly true and important utterances by Karl Kautsky on the new programme of the Austrian Social-Democratic Party: *

Many of our revisionist critics believe that Marx asserted that economic development and the class struggle create, not only the conditions for Socialist production, but also, and directly, the *consciousness* (K. K.'s italics) of its necessity. And these critics advance the argument that the most highly capitalistically developed country, England, is more remote than any other from this consciousness. Judging from the draft, one must come to the conclusion that the committee which drafted the Austrian Programme shared this alleged orthodox-Marxian view which is thus refuted. In the draft programme it is stated: "The more capitalist development increases the numbers of the proletariat, the more the proletariat is compelled, and obtains the opportunity to fight against capitalism." The proletariat becomes "conscious" of the possibility and necessity for Socialism. In this connection Socialist consciousness is represented as a necessary and direct result of the proletarian class struggle. But this is absolutely untrue. Of course, Socialism, as a theory, has its roots in a modern economic relationship in the same way as the class struggle of the proletariat has, and in the same way as the latter emerges from the struggle against the capitalist-created poverty and misery of the masses. But Socialism and the class struggle arise side by side and not one out of the other; each arises out of different premises. Modern Socialist consciousness can arise only on the basis of profound scientific knowledge. Indeed, modern economic science is as much a condition for Socialist production, as, say, modern technology, and the proletariat can create neither the one nor the other, no matter how much it may desire to do so; both arise out of the modern social process. The vehicles of science are not the proletariat, but the *bourgeois intelligentsia* (K. K.'s italics): It was out of the heads of members of this stratum that modern Socialism originated, and it was they who communicated it to the more intellectually developed proletarians who, in their turn, introduce it into the proletarian class struggle where conditions allow that to be done. Thus, Socialist consciousness is something introduced into the proletarian class struggle from without (*von Aussen Hineingetragenes*), and not something that arose within it spontaneously (*urwüchsig*). Accordingly, the old Hainfeld programme quite rightly stated that the task of Social-Democracy is to imbue the proletariat with the *consciousness* of its position and the consciousness of its tasks. There would be no need for this if consciousness emerged from the class struggle. The new draft copied this postulate from the old programme, and attached it to the postulate mentioned above. But this completely broke the line of thought. . . .

Since there can be no talk of an independent ideology being developed by the masses of the workers in the process of their move-

---

* *Neue Zeit*, 1901-1902, XX, I, No. 3, p. 79. The committee's draft to which Kautsky refers was passed by the Vienna Congress at the end of last year in a slightly amended form.

ment * then *the only choice is:* Either bourgeois, or Socialist ideology. There is no middle course (for humanity has not created a "third" ideology, and, moreover, in a society torn by class antagonisms there can never be a non-class or above-class ideology). Hence, to belittle Socialist ideology *in any way,* to *deviate from it in the slightest degree* means strengthening bourgeois ideology. There is a lot of talk about spontaneity, but the *spontaneous* development of the labour movement leads to its becoming subordinated to bourgeois ideology, it means developing *according to the programme* of the *Credo,* for the spontaneous labour movement is pure and simple trade unionism, is *Nur-Gewerkschaftlerei,* and trade unionism means the ideological subordination of the workers to the bourgeoisie. Hence, our task, the task of Social-Democracy, is to *combat spontaneity,* to *divert* the labour movement, with its spontaneous trade-unionist striving, from under the wing of the bourgeoisie, and to bring it under the wing of revolutionary Social-Democracy. The phrases employed by the authors of the "Economic" letter in *Iskra,* No. 12, about the efforts of the most inspired ideologists not being able to divert the labour movement from the path that is determined by the interaction of the material elements and the material environment *are tantamount to the abandonment of Socialism,* and if only the authors of this letter fearlessly thought out what they say to its logical conclusion, as every one who enters into the arena of literary and public activity should do, they would have nothing else to do but "fold their useless arms over their empty breasts" and . . . leave the field of action to the Struves and Prokopoviches who are dragging the labour movement "along the line of least resistance," *i. e.,* along the line of bourgeois trade

* This does not mean, of course, that the workers have no part in creating such an ideology. But they take part not as workers, but as Socialist theoreticians, like Proudhon and Weitling; in other words, they take part only to the extent that they are able, more or less, to acquire the knowledge of their age and advance that knowledge. And in order that working men *may be able to do this more often,* efforts must be made to raise the level of the consciousness of the workers generally; care must be taken that the workers do not confine themselves to the artificially restricted limits of *literature for workers* but that they study *general literature* to an increasing degree. It would even be more true to say "were not confined," instead of "not confine themselves," because the workers themselves wish to read and do read all that is written for the intelligentsia and it is only a few (bad) intellectuals who believe that it is sufficient "for the workers" to tell them a few things about factory conditions, and to repeat over and over again what has long been known.

unionism, or to the Zubatovs who are dragging it along the line of clerical and gendarme "ideology."

Recall the example of Germany. What was the historical service Lassalle rendered to the German labour movement? It was that he *diverted* that movement from the path of progressive trade unionism and co-operation, along which it was travelling spontaneously (*with the benign assistance of Schulze-Delitzsch and those like him*). To fulfil a task like that, it is necessary to do something altogether different from indulging in talk about belittling the spontaneous element, about the tactics-process and about the interaction between elements and environment, etc. *A desperate struggle against spontaneity had to be carried on*, and only after such a struggle, extending over many years, was it possible to convert the working population of Berlin from a bulwark of the Progressive Party into one of the finest strongholds of Social-Democracy. This fight is not finished even now (as those who study the history of the German movement from Prokopovich, and its philosophy from Struve believe). Even now the German working class is, so to speak, broken up into a number of ideologies. A section of the workers is organised in Catholic and Monarchist labour unions; another section is organised in the Hirsch-Duncker unions, founded by the bourgeois worshippers of English trade unionism, while a third section is organised in Social-Democratic trade unions. The latter is immeasurably more numerous than the rest, but Social-Democracy was able to achieve this superiority and will be able to maintain it, only by unswervingly fighting against all other ideologies.

But why, the reader will ask, does the spontaneous movement, the movement along the line of least resistance, lead to the domination of bourgeois ideology? For the simple reason that bourgeois ideology is far older in origin than Social-Democratic ideology; because it is more fully developed and because it possesses *immeasurably* more opportunities for becoming widespread.* And

* It is often said: The working class *spontaneously* gravitates towards Socialism. This is perfectly true in the sense that Socialist theory defines the causes of the poverty of the working class more profoundly and more correctly than any other theory, and for that reason the workers are able to appreciate it so easily, *provided*, however, that this theory does not step aside for spontaneity and *provided* it subordinates spontaneity to itself. Usually this is taken for granted, but *Rabocheye Dyelo* forgets or distorts this obvious thing. The working class spontaneously gravitates towards Socialism, nevertheless, the more widespread (and continuously revived in the most

the younger the Socialist movement is in any given country, the more vigorously must it fight against all attempts to entrench non-Socialist ideology, and the more strongly must it warn the workers against those bad counsellors who shout against "exaggerating the conscious elements," etc. The authors of the Economic Letter, in unison with *Rabocheye Dyelo*, declaim against the intolerance that is characteristic of the infancy of the movement. To this we reply: Yes, our movement is indeed in its infancy, and in order that it may grow up the quicker, it must become infected with intolerance against all those who retard its growth by subservience to spontaneity. Nothing is so ridiculous and harmful as pretending that we are "old hands" who have long ago experienced all the decisive episodes of the struggle!

Thirdly, the first number of *Rabochaya Mysl* shows that the term "Economism" (which, of course, we do not propose to abandon because it has more or less established itself) does not adequately convey the real character of the new tendency. *Rabochaya Mysl* does not altogether repudiate the political struggle: The Benefit Society constitution, published in *Rabochaya Mysl*, No. 1, contains a reference to fighting against the government. *Rabochaya Mysl* believes, however, that "politics always obediently follow economics" (and *Rabocheye Dyelo* gives a variation of this thesis when, in its programme, it asserts that "in Russia more than in any other country, the economic struggle is *inseparable* from the political struggle"). *If by politics is meant Social-Democratic politics*, then the postulates advanced by *Rabochaya Mysl* and *Rabocheye Dyelo* are wrong. The economic struggle of the workers is very often connected with (although not inseparable from) bourgeois politics, clerical politics, etc., as we have already seen. If by politics is meant trade-union politics, *i. e.*, the common striving of all workers to secure from the government measures for the alleviation of their distress, measures characteristic of their position, but which do not altogether change that position, *i. e.*, which do not remove the subjection of labour to capital, then *Rabocheye Dyelo's* postulate is correct. That striving indeed is common to the British trade unionists, who are hostile to Socialism, to the Catholic workers, to the "Zubatov" workers, etc. There are politics and politics. We see, therefore, that *Rabochaya Mysl* does not so much deny the political

diverse forms) bourgeois ideology imposes itself spontaneously upon the working class more than any other.

struggle as bow to its *spontaneity*, to its lack of purpose. While recognising the political struggle (it would be more correct to say: the political desires and demands of the workers), which arises spontaneously from the labour movement itself, it absolutely refuses *independently to work out* a specifically *Social-Democratic policy* corresponding to the general tasks of Socialism and to contemporary conditions in Russia. Farther on we shall show that *Rabocheye Dyelo* commits the same error.

C. THE SELF-EMANCIPATION GROUP AND *Rabocheye Dyelo*

We have dealt at such length with the little-known and now almost forgotten leading article in the first number of *Rabochaya Mysl* because it was the first and most striking expression of that general stream of thought which afterwards found the light of day in innumerable streamlets. V. I. was absolutely right when, in praising the first number and the leading article of *Rabochaya Mysl*, he said that it was written in a "sharp and provocative" style [*Listok Rabotnika*, Nos. 9-10, p. 49]. Every man with convictions, who thinks he has something new to say, writes "provocatively" and expresses his views strongly. Only those who are accustomed to sit between two stools lack "provocativeness"; only such people are able to praise the provocativeness of *Rabochaya Mysl* one day, and attack the "provocative polemics" of its opponents the next.

We shall not dwell on the Special Supplement to *Rabochaya Mysl* (below we shall have occasion on a number of points to refer to this work, which expresses the ideas of the Economists more consistently than any other) but shall briefly mention the *Manifesto of the Self-Emancipation of the Workers' Group* [March, 1899, reprinted in the London *Nakanunye* [*On the Eve*], No. 7, June, 1899]. The authors of this manifesto quite rightly say that "the workers of Russia *are only just awakening*, are only just looking around, and *instinctively clutch at the first means of struggle that come to their hands.*" But from this correct observation, they draw the same incorrect conclusion that is drawn by *Rabochaya Mysl*, forgetting that instinct is that unconsciousness (spontaneity) to whose aid the Socialists must come; that the "first means of struggle that come to their hands" will always be in modern society, the trade union means of struggle, and the "first ideology that comes to hand" will be bourgeois (trade union) ideology. Similarly, these authors do not "repudiate" politics, they merely say (merely!), repeating what was said by V. V., that politics are the superstructure, and therefore, "political agitation must be the superstructure to the agitation carried on in favour of the economic struggle; it must arise on the basis of this struggle and give precedence to it."

As for *Rabocheye Dyelo*, it commenced its activity by "a defence" of the Economists. It uttered *a downright untruth* in its very first number [No. 1, pp. 141-142] when it stated that it "did not know which young comrades Axelrod referred to" in his well-known pamphlet, in which he uttered a warning against the Economists.* In the controversy that flared up with Axelrod and Plekhanov over this falsehood, *Rabocheye Dyelo* was compelled to admit that "by expressing ignorance, it desired to *defend* all the younger Social-Democrats abroad from this unjust accusation" (Axelrod accused the Economists of having a restricted outlook). As a matter of fact this accusation was absolutely just, and *Rabocheye Dyelo* knows perfectly well that, among others, it applied to V. I., a member of its editorial staff. We shall observe in passing that in this controversy Axelrod was absolutely right, and *Rabocheye Dyelo* was absolutely wrong, in their respective interpretations of my pamphlet: *The Tasks of Russian Social-Democrats.*** That pamphlet was written in 1897, before the appearance of *Rabochaya Mysl* when I thought, and rightly thought, that the *original* tendency of the St. Petersburg League of Struggle, which I described above, was the predominant one. At all events, that tendency was the predominant one until the middle of 1898. Consequently, in its attempt to refute the existence and dangers of Economism, *Rabocheye Dyelo* had no right whatever to refer to a pamphlet which expressed views that were *squeezed out* by Economist views in St. Petersburg in 1897-1898.***

* *The Contemporary Tasks and Tactics of the Russian Social-Democrats,* Geneva, 1898. Two letters written to *Rabochaya Gazeta* in 1897.

** See V. I. Lenin, *Collected Works*, Vol. II.—*Ed.*

*** In its attempt to justify the first untruth it uttered ("we do not know which young comrades Axelrod referred to") *Rabocheye Dyelo* uttered a second, when, in its *Reply* it wrote: "Since the review of *The Tasks* was published, a tendency has arisen, or has become more or less defined among certain Russian Social-Democrats, towards economic one-sidedness, which represents a step backwards from the state of our movement as described in *The Tasks*" [p. 9]. This is what the *Reply* says, *published in 1900.* But the first number of *Rabocheye Dyelo* (containing the review) appeared *in April, 1899.* Did Economism arise only in 1899? No. The protest of the

But *Rabocheye Dyelo* not only "defended" the Economists—it itself constantly fell into fundamental Economist errors. The cause of these errors is to be found in the ambiguity of the interpretation given to the following thesis in *Rabocheye Dyelo's* programme: "We consider that the most important phenomenon of Russian life, the one that will mostly *determine the tasks* [our italics] and the character of the literary activity of the league, is the *mass labour movement* [*Rabocheye Dyelo's* italics] that has arisen in recent years." That the mass movement is a most important phenomenon is a fact about which there can be no dispute. But the crux of the question is, What is the meaning of the phrase: The labour movement will "determine the tasks"? It may be interpreted in one of two ways. *Either* it means subservience to the spontaneity of this movement, *i. e.*, reducing the rôle of Social-Democracy to mere subservience to the labour movement as such (the interpretation given to it by *Rabochaya Mysl,* the Self-Emancipation group and other Economists) ; *or* it may mean that the mass movement sets before us *new*, theoretical, political and organisational tasks, far more complicated than those that might have satisfied us in the period before the rise of the mass movement. *Rabocheye Dyelo* inclined and still inclines towards the first interpretation, for it said nothing definitely about new tasks, but argued all the time as if the "mass movement" *relieved* us of the necessity of clearly appreciating and fulfilling the tasks it sets before us. We need only point out that *Rabocheye Dyelo* considered that we could not possibly accept the overthrow of the autocracy as the *first* task of the mass labour movement, and that it degraded this task (ostensibly in the interests of the mass movement) to the struggle for immediate political demands. [*Reply,* p. 25.]

We shall pass over the article by B. Krichevsky, the editor of *Rabocheye Dyelo,* entitled "The Economic and Political Struggle in the Russian Movement," published in No. 7, of that paper, in which these very mistakes are repeated * and take up *Rabocheye Dyelo,* No. 10.

Russian Social-Democrats against Economism (the protest against the *Credo*) appeared in 1899. Economism arose in 1897, as *Rabocheye Dyelo* very well knows, for *already in November, 1898,* V. I. praised *Rabochaya Mysl,* in *Listok Rabotnika,* Nos. 9-10.

* The "stages theory," or the theory of "timid zigzags" in the political struggle, is expressed in this article approximately in the following way:

We shall not, of course, enter in detail into the various objections raised by B. Krichevsky and Martynov against *Zarya* and *Iskra*. What interests us here solely, is the theoretical position taken up by *Rabocheye Dyelo*, No. 10. For example, we shall not examine the literary curiosity, that *Rabocheye Dyelo* saw a "diametrical" contradiction between the postulate:

> Social-Democracy does not tie its hands, it does not restrict its activities to some preconceived plan or method of political struggle: It recognises all methods of struggle, as long as they correspond to the forces at the disposal of the party . . . under the given conditions, etc. [*Iskra*, No. 1].*

and the postulate:

> Without a strong organisation, tested in the political struggle carried on under all circumstances and in all periods, there can be no talk of a systematic plan of activity, enlightened by firm principles and unswervingly carried out, which alone is worthy of being called tactics [*Iskra*, No. 4].**

To confuse the recognition, *in principle*, of all means of struggle, of all plans and methods, provided they are expedient—with the necessity *at a given political moment*, to be guided by a strictly adhered to plan in talking of tactics, is tantamount to confusing the

"Political demands, which in their character are common to the whole of Russia should, however, at first [this was written in August, 1900!] correspond to the experience gained by the given stratum [*sic!*] of workers in the economic struggle. Only [!] on the basis of this experience can and should the political agitation be taken up," etc. [p. 11]. On page 4, the author, protesting against what he regards as the absolutely unfounded charge of Economist heresy, pathetically exclaims: "What Social-Democrat does not know that according to the theories of Marx and Engels, the class interest is the decisive factor in history, and, *consequently*, that the proletarian struggle for the defence of its economic interests must be of first-rate importance in its class development and struggle for emancipation?" (our italics). The word "consequently" is absolutely out of place. The fact that economic interests are a decisive factor *does not in the least imply* that the economic (*i. e.*, trade union) struggle must be the main factor, for the essential and "decisive" interest of classes can be satisfied *only* by radical *political* changes. In particular the fundamental economic interests of the proletariat can be satisfied only by a political revolution, that will substitute the dictatorship of the proletariat for the dictatorship of the bourgeoisie. B. Krichevsky repeats the arguments of the "V. V.'s of Russian Social-Democracy" (*i. e.*, politics follows economics, etc.), and the Bernsteinists of German Social-Democracy (for example, by arguments like these, Woltmann tried to prove that the workers must first of all acquire "economic power" before they can think about political revolution).

* See conclusion of article, "The Urgent Tasks of Our Movement," *The Iskra Period*, Book I, p. 57.—*Ed.*

** See beginning of article "Where to Begin," *The Iskra Period*, Book I, p. 109.—*Ed.*

recognition by medical science of all kinds of treatment of diseases with the necessity for adopting a certain definite method of treatment for a given disease. The point is, however, that *Rabocheye Dyelo*, while suffering from a disease which we have called subservience to spontaneity, refuses to recognise any "method of treatment" for *that* disease. Hence, it made the remarkable discovery that "a plan of tactics contradicts the fundamental spirit of Marxism" [No. 10, p. 18], that tactics are *"a process of growth of party tasks, which grow with the party"* [(p. 11), *Rabocheye Dyelo's* italics]. The latter remark has every chance of becoming a celebrated maxim, a permanent monument to the tendency of *Rabocheye Dyelo*. To the question: *Whither?* a leading organ replies: Motion is a process of alteration in the distance between starting point and destination. This matchless example of profundity is not merely a literary curiosity (if it were, it would not be worth dealing with at length), but *the programme of the whole tendency, i. e.,* the programme which R. M. (in the Special Supplement to *Rabochaya Mysl*) expressed in the words: "That struggle is desirable which is possible, and the struggle which is possible is the one that is going on now." It is the tendency of unbounded opportunism, which passively adapts itself to spontaneity.

"A plan of tactics contradicts the fundamental spirit of Marxism!" But this is a libel on Marxism; it is like the caricature of it that was presented to us by the Narodniks in their fight against us. It means putting restraint on the initiative and energy of class-conscious fighters, whereas Marxism, on the contrary, gives a gigantic impetus to the initiative and energy of Social-Democrats, opens up for them the widest perspectives and, if one may so express it, places at their disposal the mighty force of millions and millions of workers "spontaneously" rising for the struggle. The whole history of international Social-Democracy seethes with plans advanced first by one and then by another political leader; some confirming the far-sightedness and correct political and organisational insight of their authors and others revealing their short-sightedness and lack of political judgment. At the time when Germany was passing one of the most important turning points in its history—the time of the establishment of the Empire, the opening of the Reichstag, and the granting of universal suffrage, Liebknecht had one plan for Social-Democratic policy and work, and Schweitzer had another.

When the anti-Socialist laws came down on the heads of the German Socialists, Most and Hasselmann, had one plan, that is, to call for violence and terror; Höchberg, Schramm and (partly) Bernstein had another, which they began to preach to the Social-Democrats, somewhat as follows: They themselves provoked the passing of the anti-Socialist laws by being unreasonably bitter and revolutionary, and must now show that they deserve pardon by exemplary conduct. There was yet a third plan proposed by those who paved the way for and carried out the publication of an illegal organ. It is easy, of course, in retrospect, many years after the fight over the selection of the path to be followed has finished, and after history has pronounced its verdict as to the expediency of the path selected, to utter profound maxims about the growth of party tasks that grow with the party. But at a time of confusion,* when the Russian "critics" and Economists degrade Social-Democracy to the level of trade unionism, and when the terrorists are strongly advocating the adoption of a "plan of tactics" that repeats the old mistakes, at such a time, to confine oneself to such profundities, means simply to issue to oneself a "certificate of mental poverty." At a time when many Russian Social-Democrats suffer from lack of initiative and energy, from a lack of "breadth of political propaganda, agitation and organisation,** a lack of plans for a broader organisation of revolutionary work, at such a time to say: "A plan of tactics contradicts the fundamental spirit of Marxism," not only means theoretically to vulgarise Marxism, but also practically to *drag the party backward*. *Rabocheye Dyelo* goes on sermonising:

The revolutionary Social-Democrat is only confronted by the task of accelerating objective development by his conscious work; it is not his task to obviate it or substitute his own subjective plans for this development. *Iskra* knows all this in theory. But the enormous importance which Marxism quite justly attaches to conscious revolutionary work causes it in practice, owing to its doctrinaire view of tactics, to *belittle the significance of the objective or the spontaneous elements of development* [p. 18].

Another example of the extraordinary theoretical confusion worthy of V. V. and that fraternity. We would ask our philosopher:

* *Ein Jahr Der Verwirrung* (*A Year of Confusion*) is the title Mehring gave to the chapter of his *History of German Social-Democracy* in which he describes the hesitancy and lack of determination displayed at first by the Socialists in selecting the "plan of tactics" for the new situation.
** See leading article in *Iskra*, No. 1, "The Urgent Tasks of our Movement," *The Iskra Period*, Book I, p. 53.—*Ed.*

How may a deviser of subjective plans "belittle" objective development? Obviously by losing sight of the fact that this objective development creates or strengthens, destroys or weakens certain classes, strata, groups, nations, groups of nations, etc., and in this way creates a definite international, political grouping of forces, the position of revolutionary parties, etc. If the deviser of plans did that, his mistake would not be that he belittled the spontaneous element, but that he belittled the *conscious element*, for he would then show that he lacked the "consciousness" that would enable him properly to understand objective development. Hence, the very talk about "estimating the *relative* significance" (*Rabocheye Dyelo's* italics) of spontaneity and consciousness sufficiently reveals a complete lack of "consciousness." If certain "spontaneous elements of development" can be grasped at all by human understanding, then an incorrect estimation of them would be tantamount to "belittling the conscious element." But if they cannot be grasped, then we cannot be aware of them, and therefore cannot speak of them. What is B. Krichevsky arguing about then? If he thinks that *Iskra's* "subjective plans" are erroneous (as he in fact declares them to be), then he ought to show what objective facts are ignored in these plans, and then charge *Iskra* with *a lack of consciousness* for ignoring them, with, to use his own words, "belittling the conscious element." If, however, while being displeased with subjective plans he can bring forward no other argument except that of "belittling the spontaneous element" (!!) he merely shows: 1. That he theoretically understands Marxism à la Kareyevs and the Mikhailovskys, who have been sufficiently ridiculed by Beltov, and 2. That practically, he is quite pleased with the "spontaneous elements of development" that have drawn our legal Marxists towards Bernsteinism and our Social-Democrats towards Economism, and that he is full of wrath against those who have determined at all costs to *divert* Russian Social-Democracy from the path of spontaneous development.

And then follow things that are positively funny. "In the same way as men and women will multiply in the old-fashioned way, notwithstanding all the discoveries of natural science, so the birth of a new social order will come about in the future *mainly* as a result of elemental outbursts, notwithstanding all the discoveries of social science and the increase in the number of conscious fighters." [p. 19.] Our grandfathers, in their old-fashioned wisdom used to say: "Any fool can bring forth children," and to-day the "modern Socialists" (à la Narcissus Tuporylov) in their wisdom say: "Any fool can help the spontaneous birth of a new social order." We too are of that opinion. All that is required for help of that kind is to *surrender* to Economism when Economism reigns and to terrorism when terrorism arises. For example, in the spring of this year, when it was so important to utter a note of warning against terrorism, *Rabocheye Dyelo* stood in amazement confronted by a problem that was "new" to it and now, six months after, when the problem has become less topical, it, at one and the same time, presents us with the declaration: "We think that it is not and cannot be the task of Social-Democracy to counteract the rise of terroristic temper" [*Rabocheye Dyelo*, No. 10, p. 23], and the congress resolution: "The congress regards systematic and aggressive terror as being inopportune" [*Two Congresses,* p. 18]. How beautifully clear and connected this is! Not to counteract, but to declare inopportune, and to declare it in such a way that the "resolution" shall not apply to unsystematic and defencive terror. It must be admitted that a resolution like that is extremely safe and completely insured against error, just as a man who talks, but says nothing, is insured against error! And all that is required to be able to draft a resolution like that is: Ability to keep *at the tail end* of the movement. When *Iskra* ridiculed *Rabocheye Dyelo* for declaring the question of terror to be a new one,* the latter angrily accused *Iskra* of "having the incredible effrontery to impose upon the party organisations decisions on tactical questions arrived at by a group of emigrant writers more than sixteen years ago" [p. 24]. Effrontery indeed, and an exaggeration of the conscious elements *to* find the theoretical solutions to problems, and then to try to prove to the organisation, to the party and to the masses that this solution is correct! ** How much better it is to repeat something that has been learned by rote, and, without "imposing" anything upon anybody, swing with every "turn" in the direction of Economism or in the direction of terrorism. *Rabocheye Dyelo* even goes so far as to generalise this gospel of worldly wisdom and accuses

* See beginning of article "Where to Begin," *The Iskra Period,* Book I, p. 109.—*Ed.*
** Nor must it be forgotten that in solving "theoretically" the problem of terror, the Emancipation of Labour group *generalised* the experience of the preceding revolutionary movement.

Iskra and *Zarya* with "setting up its programme against the move-ment, like a spirit hovering over the formless chaos" (p. 29). But what else is the function of Social-Democracy if not to be a "spirit," not only hovering over the spontaneous movement but also *raising* the movement *to the level of "its programme"?* Surely, it is not its function to drag at the *tail* of the movement: At best, this would be of no service to the movement; at the worst, it would be very, very harmful. *Rabocheye Dyelo*, however, not only follows this "tactics-process," but elevates it to a principle, so that it would be more correct to describe its tendency not as opportunism, but *khvostism* (from the word *khvost*).* And it must be admitted, that those who have determined always to follow behind the movement like a tail, are absolutely and forever ensured against "belittling the spon-taneous element of development."

And so, we have become convinced that the fundamental error committed by the "new tendency" in Russian Social-Democracy lies in its subservience to spontaneity, and its failure to understand that the spontaneity of the masses demands a mass of consciousness from us Social-Democrats. The more spontaneously the masses rise, the more widespread the movement becomes, so much the more rapidly grows the demand for greater consciousness in the theoretical, political and organisational work of Social-Democracy.

The spontaneous rise of the masses in Russia proceeded (and continues) with such rapidity that the young untrained Social-Democrats proved unfitted for the gigantic tasks that confronted them. This lack of training is our common misfortune, the mis-fortune of *all* Russian Social-Democrats. The rise of the masses proceeded and spread uninterruptedly and continuously; it not only continued in the places it commenced in, but it spread to new locali-ties and to new strata of the population (influenced by the labour movement, the ferment among the students and the intellectuals generally, and even among the peasantry revived). Revolution-aries, however, *lagged behind* this rise of the masses in both their "theories" and in their practical activity; they failed to establish an uninterrupted organisation having continuity with the past, and capable of *leading* the whole movement.

In Chapter I, we proved that *Rabocheye Dyelo* degraded our theoretical tasks and that it "spontaneously" repeated the fashion-

* *Khvost* is the Russian word for tail.—*Ed.*

able catchword "freedom of criticism": that those who repeated this catchword lacked the "consciousness" to understand that the position of the opportunist "critics" and the revolutionaries, both in Germany and in Russia, are diametrically opposed to each other.

In the following chapters, we shall show how this subservience to spontaneity found expression in the sphere of the political tasks and the organisational work of Social-Democracy.

III

TRADE-UNION POLITICS AND SOCIAL-DEMOCRATIC POLITICS

WE shall start off again from the praises that have been sung for *Rabocheye Dyelo*. Martynov gave his article in No. 10 of *Rabocheye Dyelo*, on his differences with *Iskra*, the title: "Exposure Literature and the Proletarian Struggle." He formulated the substance of these differences as follows:

We cannot confine ourselves entirely to exposing the state of affairs that stand in its [the labour party's] path of development. We must also respond to the immediate and current interests of the proletariat [p. 63].

". . . *Iskra* . . . is in fact the organ of revolutionary opposition that exposes the state of affairs in our country, particularly the political state of affairs. . . . We, however, work and shall continue to work for the cause of labour in close organic contact with the proletarian struggle" [*ibid.*]. One cannot help being grateful to Martynov for this formula. It is of exceptional general interest because substantially it embraces not only our disagreements with *Rabocheye Dyelo*, but the general disagreement between ourselves and the Economists concerning the political struggle. We have shown already that the Economists do not altogether repudiate "politics," but that they are constantly deviating from the Social-Democratic conception of politics to the trade-unionist conception. Martynov deviates in exactly the same way, and we agree, therefore, to take him as an *example* of an Economist wandering into error on this question. As we shall endeavour to prove, neither the authors of the Special Supplement of *Rabochaya Mysl*, nor the authors of the manifesto issued by the Emancipation group, nor the authors of the Economist Letter published in *Iskra*, No. 12, will have any right to complain against this choice.

A. POLITICAL AGITATION AND ITS RESTRICTION BY THE ECONOMISTS

Every one knows that the spread and consolidation of the economic * struggle of the Russian workers proceeded simultaneously

* In order to avoid misunderstanding we would state, that here, and throughout this pamphlet, by economic struggle, we mean (in accordance with

with the creation of a "literature" exposing economic conditions, *i. e.*, factory and industrial conditions. These "leaflets" were devoted mainly to the exposure of factory conditions, and very soon a passion for exposures was roused among the workers. As soon as the workers realised that the Social-Democratic circles desired to and could supply them with a new kind of leaflet that told the whole truth about their poverty-stricken lives, about their excessive toil and their lack of rights, correspondence began to pour in from the factories and workshops. This "exposure literature" created a sensation not only in the particular factory dealt with and the conditions of which were exposed in a given leaflet, but in all the factories to which news had spread about the facts exposed. And as the poverty and want among the workers in the various enterprises and in the various trades are pretty much the same, the "Truth about the life of the workers" roused the admiration *of all*. Even among the most backward workers, a veritable passion was roused to "go into print"—a noble passion to adopt this rudimentary form of war against the whole of the modern social system which is based upon robbery and oppression. And in the overwhelming majority of cases these "leaflets" were in truth a declaration of war, because the exposures had a terrifically rousing effect upon the workers; it stimulated them to put forward demands for the removal of the most glaring evils, and roused in them a readiness to support these demands with strikes. Finally, the employers themselves were compelled to recognise the significance of these leaflets as a declaration of war, so much so that in a large number of cases they did not even wait for the outbreak of hostilities. As is always the case, the mere publication of these exposures made them effective, and they acquired the significance of a strong moral force. On more than one occasion, the mere appearance of a leaflet proved sufficient to compel an employer to concede all or part of the demands put forward. In a word, economic (factory) exposures have been an important lever in the economic struggle and they will continue to be so as long as capitalism, which creates the need for the workers to defend themselves, exists. Even in the more progressive countries of Europe to-day, the exposure of the evils in some backward

the meaning of the term as it has become accepted amongst us) the "practical economic struggle" which Engels, in the passage we quoted above, described as "resistance to capitalism," and which in free countries is known as the trade-union struggle.

trade, or in some forgotten branch of domestic industry, serves as a starting point for the awakening of class-consciousness, for the beginning of a trade-union struggle, and for the spread of Socialism.*

Recently, the overwhelming majority of Russian Social-Democrats were almost wholly engaged in this work of exposing factory conditions. It is sufficient to refer to the columns of *Rabochaya Mysl* to judge to what an extent they were engaged in it. So much so indeed, that they lost sight of the fact that this, *taken by itself*, was not substantially Social-Democratic work, but merely trade-union work. As a matter of fact, these exposures merely dealt with the relations between the workers *in a given trade*, with their immediate employers, and all that it achieved was that the vendors of labour power learned to sell their "commodity" on better terms, and to fight the purchasers of labour power over a purely commercial deal. These exposures might have served (if properly utilised by revolutionaries) as a beginning and a constituent part of Social-Democratic activity, but they might also (and with subservience to spontaneity inevitably had to) have led to a "pure and simple" trade-union struggle and to a non-Social-Democratic labour movement. Social-Democrats lead the struggle of the working class not only for better terms for the sale of labour power, but also for the abolition of the social system which compels the propertyless class to sell itself to the rich. Social-Democracy represents the working class, not in its relation to a given group of employers, but in its relation to all classes in modern society, to the state as an organised political force. Hence, it not only follows that Social-Democrats must not

---

* In the present chapter, we deal only with the *political* struggle; *i. e.*, whether it is to be understood in its broader or narrower sense. Therefore, we refer only in passing, merely to point out a curiosity, to the accusation that *Rabocheye Dyelo* hurls against *Iskra* of being "too restrained" in regard to the economic struggle [*Two Congresses*, p. 27, rehashed by Martynov in his pamphlet: *Social-Democracy and the Working Class*]. If those who make this accusation counted up in terms of hundredweights or reams, as they are so fond of doing, what has been said about the economic struggle in the industrial column of *Iskra* in one year's issue, and compared this with the industrial columns of *Rabocheye Dyelo* and *Rabochaya Mysl* taken together, they would see that they lag very much behind even in this respect. Apparently, the consciousness of this simple truth compels them to resort to arguments which clearly reveal their confusion. "*Iskra*," they write, "willy-nilly [!] is compelled [!] to take note of the imperative demands of life and to publish at least [!!!] correspondence about the labour movement" [*Two Congresses*, p. 27]. Now this is really a crushing argument!

confine themselves entirely to the economic struggle; they must not even allow the organisation of economic exposures to become the predominant part of their activities. We must actively take up the political education of the working class, and the development of its political consciousness. *Now,* after *Zarya* and *Iskra* have made the first attack upon Economism "all are agreed" with this (although some agreed only nominally, as we shall soon prove).

The question now arises: What does political education mean? Is it sufficient to confine oneself to the propaganda of working-class hostility to autocracy? Of course not. It is not enough to *explain* to the workers that they are politically oppressed (any more than it was to *explain* to them that their interests were antagonistic to the interests of the employers). Advantage must be taken of every concrete example of this oppression for the purpose of agitation (in the same way as we began to use concrete examples of economic oppression for the purpose of agitation). And inasmuch as *political* oppression affects all sorts of classes in society, inasmuch as it manifests itself in various spheres of life and activity, in industrial life, civic life, in personal and family life, in religious life, scientific life, etc., etc., is it not evident that *we shall not be fulfilling our task* of developing the political consciousness of the workers if *we do not undertake* the organisation of the *political exposure of autocracy in all its aspects?* In order to agitate over concrete examples of oppression, these examples must be exposed (in the same way as it was necessary to expose factory evils in order to carry on economic agitation).

One would think that this was clear enough. It turns out, however, that "all" are agreed that it is necessary to develop political consciousness *in all its aspects,* only in words. It turns out that *Rabocheye Dyelo,* for example, has not only failed to take up the task of organising (or to make a start in organising) in all-sided political exposure, but is even trying to *drag Iskra,* which has undertaken this task, *away from it.* Listen to this: "The political struggle of the working class is merely [it is precisely not "merely"] a more developed, a wider and more effective form of economic struggle." [Programme of *Rabocheye Dyelo* published in No. 1, p. 3.] "The Social-Democrats are now confronted with the task of, as far as possible, giving the economic struggle itself a political character" [Martynov, *Rabocheye Dyelo,* No. 10, p. 42]. "The economic struggle is the most widely applicable method of drawing the masses into active political struggle" (resolution passed by the congress of the League and "amendments" thereto). [*Two Congresses*, pp. 11 and 17]. As the reader will observe, all these postulates permeate *Rabocheye Dyelo*, from its very first number to the recently issued Instructions by the Editorial Committee, and all of them evidently express a single view regarding political agitation and the political struggle. Examine this view from the standpoint of the opinion prevailing among all Economists, that political agitation must *follow* economic agitation. Is it true that in general,* the economic struggle "is the most widely applicable method" of drawing the masses into the political struggle? It is absolutely untrue. All and sundry manifestations of police tyranny and autocratic outrage, in addition to the evils connected with the economic struggle, are equally "widely applicable" as a means of "drawing in" the masses. The tyranny of the Zemstvo chiefs, the flogging of the peasantry, the corruption of the officials, the conduct of the police towards the "common people" in the cities, the fight against the famine-stricken and the suppression of the popular striving towards enlightenment and knowledge, the extortion of taxes, the persecution of the religious sects, the severe discipline in the army, the militarist conduct towards the students and the liberal intelligentsia—all these and a thousand other similar manifestations of tyranny, though not directly connected with the "economic" struggle, do they, in general, represent a *less* "widely applicable" method and subject for political agitation and for drawing the masses into the political struggle? The very opposite is the case. Of all the innumerable cases in which the workers suffer (either personally or those closely associated with them) from tyranny, violence, and lack of rights, undoubtedly only a relatively few represent cases of police tyranny in the economic struggle as such. Why then should we beforehand *restrict* the scope of political agitation by declaring *only one* of the

* We say "in general," advisedly, because *Rabocheye Dyelo* speaks of general principles and of the general tasks of the whole party. Undoubtedly, cases occur in practice, when politics *must* follow economics, but only Economists can say a thing like that in a resolution that was intended to apply to the whole of Russia. Cases do occur when it is possible "right from the beginning," to carry on political agitation "exclusively on an economic basis"; and yet *Rabocheye Dyelo* went so far as to say that "there was no need for this whatever" [*Two Congresses*, p. 11]. In the next chapter, we shall show that the tactics of the "politicians" and revolutionaries not only do not ignore the trade-union tasks of Social-Democracy, but that, on the contrary, they alone *can secure* the consistent fulfilment of these tasks.

methods to be "the most widely applicable," when Social-Democrats have other, generally speaking, not less "widely applicable" means? Long, long ago (a year ago! . . .) *Rabocheye Dyelo* wrote:

The masses begin to understand immediate political demands after one, or at all events, after several strikes; immediately the government sets the police and gendarmerie against them [No. 7, p. 15, August, 1900].

This opportunist theory of stages has now been rejected by the League, which makes a concession to us by declaring: "There is no need whatever to conduct political agitation right from the beginning, exclusively on an economic basis." [*Two Congresses*, p. 11.] This very repudiation of part of its former errors by the League will enable the future historian of Russian Social-Democracy to discern the depths to which our Economists have degraded Socialism better than any number of lengthy arguments! But the League must be very naïve indeed to imagine that the abandonment of one form of restricting politics will induce us to agree to another form of restriction! Would it not be more logical to say that the economic struggle should be conducted on the widest possible basis, that it should be utilised for political agitation, but that "there is no need whatever" to regard the economic struggle as the *most* widely applicable means of drawing the masses into active political struggle?

The League attaches significance to the fact that it substituted the phrase "most widely applicable method" by the phrase "a better method," contained in one of the resolutions of the Fourth Congress of the Jewish Labour League (Bund). We confess that we find it difficult to say which of these resolutions is the better one. In our opinion *both are bad*. Both the League and the Bund fall into error (partly perhaps unconsciously, owing to the influence of tradition) concerning the economic, trade-unionist interpretation of politics. The fact that this error is expressed either by the word "better" or by the words "most widely applicable" makes no material difference whatever. If the League had said that "political agitation on an economic basis" is the most widely applied (and not "applicable") method it would have been right in regard to a certain period in the development of our Social-Democratic movement. It would have been right in regard to the *Economists and to many* (if not the majority) of the practical Economists of 1898-1901 who have *applied* the method of political agitation (to the extent that they applied it at all) *almost exclusively on an economic basis.* Political agitation on *such* lines was recognised, and as we have seen, even recommended by *Rabochaya Mysl,* and by the Self-Emancipation group! *Rabocheye Dyelo* should have *strongly condemned* the fact that useful economic agitation was accompanied by the harmful restriction of the political struggle, but instead of that, it declares the method most widely *applied* (*by the Economists*) to be the most widely *applicable!* It is not surprising, therefore, that when we describe these people as Economists, they can do nothing else but pour abuse upon us, and call us "mystifiers," "disrupters," "Papal Nuncios," and "slanderers," * go complaining to the world that we have mortally offended them and declare almost on oath that "not a single Social-Democratic organisation is now tinged with Economism.** Oh, these evil, slanderous politicians! They must have deliberately invented this Economism, out of sheer hatred of mankind, in order mortally to offend other people!

What do the words "to give the economic struggle itself a political character," which Martynov uses in presenting the tasks of Social-Democracy, mean concretely? The economic struggle is the collective struggle of the workers against their employers for better terms *in the sale of their labour power,* for better conditions of life and labour. This struggle is necessarily a struggle according to trade, because conditions of labour differ very much in different trades, and, consequently, the fight to *improve* these conditions can only be conducted in respect of each trade (trade unions in the Western countries, temporary trade associations and leaflets in Russia, etc.). To give "the economic struggle itself a political character" means, therefore, to strive to secure satisfaction for these trade demands, the improvement of conditions of labour in each separate trade by means of "legislative and administrative measures" (as Martynov expresses it on the next page of his article, p. 43). This is exactly what the trade unions do and always have done. Read the works of the thoroughly scientific (and "thoroughly" opportunist) Mr. and Mrs. Webb and you will find that the British trade unions long ago recognised, and have long carried out the task of "giving the economic struggle itself a political character"; they have long been fighting for the right to strike, for the removal of all juridical hindrances to the co-operative and trade-union movement, for laws protecting women and children, for the im-

---

* These are exactly the expressions used in *Two Congresses,* pp. 28, 30, 31, and 32.

** *Two Congresses,* p. 32.

provement of conditions of labour by means of sanitary and factory legislation, etc.

Thus, the pompous phrase: "To give the economic struggle *itself* a political character," which sounds so "terrifically" profound and revolutionary, serves as a screen to conceal what is in fact the traditional striving to *degrade* Social-Democratic politics to the level of trade-union politics! On the pretext of rectifying *Iskra's* one-sidedness, which, it is alleged, places "the revolutionising of dogma higher than the revolutionising of life," * we are presented with the *struggle for economic reform* as if it were something entirely new. As a matter of fact, the phrase "to give the economic struggle itself a political character" means nothing more than the struggle for economic reforms. And Martynov himself might have come to this simple conclusion had he only pondered over the significance of his own words. "Our party," he says, turning his heaviest guns against *Iskra*, "could and should have presented concrete demands to the government for legislative and administrative measures against economic exploitation, for the relief of unemployment, for the relief of the famine-stricken, etc." [*Rabocheye Dyelo*, No. 10, pp. 42, 43.] Concrete demands for measures—does not this mean demands for social reforms? And again we ask the impartial reader, do we slander the *Rabocheye Dyeloists* (may I be forgiven for this clumsy expression!) when we declare them to be concealed Bernsteinists, for advancing their thesis about the necessity for fighting for economic reforms as a reason for their *disagreement* with *Iskra?*

Revolutionary Social-Democracy always included, and now includes, the fight for reforms in its activities. But it utilises "economic" agitation for the purpose of presenting to the government, not only demands for all sorts of measures, but also (and primarily) the demand that it cease to be an autocratic government. Moreover, it considers it to be its duty to present this demand to the government, not on the basis of the economic struggle *alone,* but on the basis of all manifestations of public and political life. In a word, it subordinates the struggle for reforms to the revolutionary struggle for liberty and for Socialism, in the same way as the part

* *Rabocheye Dyelo*, No. 10, p. 60. This is the Martynov variation of the application to the present chaotic state of our movement of the thesis: "A step forward of the real movement is more important than a dozen programmes," to which we have already referred above. As a matter of fact, this is merely a translation into Russian of the notorious Bernsteinist phrase: "The movement is everything, the ultimate aim is nothing."

is subordinate to the whole. Martynov, however, resuscitates the theory of stages in a new form, and strives to prescribe an exclusively economic, so to speak, path of development for the political struggle. By coming out at this moment, when the revolutionary movement is on the up-grade, with an alleged special "task" of fighting for reforms, he is dragging the party backwards, and is playing into the hands of both "economic" and liberal opportunism.

Shamefacedly hiding the struggle for reforms behind the pompous thesis "to give the economic struggle itself a political character," Martynov advanced, as if it were a special point, *exclusively economic* (in fact, exclusively factory) *reforms*. Why he did that, we do not know. Perhaps it was due to carelessness? But if he indeed had only "factory" reforms in mind, then the whole of his thesis, which we have just quoted, loses all sense. Perhaps he did it because he thought it possible and probable that the government would agree to make "concessions" only in the economic sphere? * If that is what he thought, then it is a strange error. Concessions are also possible, and are made in the sphere of legislation concerning flogging, passports, land-compensation payments, religious sects, the censorship, etc., etc. "Economic" concessions (or pseudo-concessions) are, of course, the cheapest and most advantageous concessions to make from the government's point-of-view, because by these means it hopes to win the confidence of the masses of the workers. Precisely for this very reason, Social-Democrats *must under no circumstances* create grounds for the belief (or the misunderstanding) that we attach greater value to economic reforms than to political reforms, or that we regard them as being particularly important, etc. "Such demands," writes Martynov, concerning the concrete demands for legislative and administrative measures referred to above, "would not be merely a hollow sound because, promising certain palpable results, they might be actively supported by the masses of the workers. . . ." We are not Economists, oh, no! We only cringe as slavishly before the "palpableness" of concrete results as do the Bernsteins, the Prokopoviches, the Struves, the R. M.'s, and *tutti quanti!* We only wish to make it understood (with Narcissus Tuporylov) that all that which "does not promise palpable results" is merely a "hollow sound." We are only trying to argue as if the

---

* P. 43. "Of course, when we advise the workers to present certain economic demands to the government, we do so because in the *economic* sphere, the autocratic government is compelled to agree to make certain concessions."

masses of the workers are incapable (and, of course, have not proved their capabilities, notwithstanding those who ascribe their own philistinism to them) of actively supporting *every* protest against the autocracy even if *it promises absolutely no palpable results whatever!*

Take for example the very "measures" for the relief of unemployment and the famine that Martynov himself advances. While *Rabocheye Dyelo* was engaged, judging by what it has promised, in drawing up a programme of "concrete [in the form of Acts of Legislation?] demands for legislative and administrative measures," "promising palpable results," *Iskra*, which "constantly places the revolutionising of dogma higher than the revolutionising of life," tried to explain the inseparable connection that exists between unemployment and the capitalist system as a whole; uttered the warning that "famine is coming"; exposed the police "fight against the famine-stricken" and the outrageous "provisional penal regulations"; and *Zarya* published a special edition in the form of an agitation pamphlet, entitled, *Review of Internal Affairs*, a part of its text which was devoted to the famine. But good God! How "one-sided" these incorrigibly narrow and orthodox doctrinaires were in this; how deaf to the calls of "life itself"! Not one of these articles contained—oh horror!—a single, can you imagine it?—*a single* "concrete demand," "promising palpable results"! Poor doctrinaires! They sought to be sent to Krichevsky and Martynov to be taught that tactics are a process of growth, etc., and that the economic struggle *itself* should be given a political character!

In addition to its immediately revolutionary significance, the workers' economic struggle against the employers and the government ["*economic* struggle against the government"!!] has also this significance that it constantly brings the workers face to face with their own lack of political rights [Martynov, p. 44].

We quote this passage not in order to repeat what has been said already a hundred and a thousand times before, but in order to thank Martynov for this excellent new formula: "The workers' economic struggle against the employers and the government." What a pearl! With what inimitable talent and skill in eliminating partial disagreements and shades of differences among Economists, does this clear and concise postulate express the *quintessence* of Economism: From calling to the workers to join "in the political struggle which they carry on in the general interest, for the purpose of improving the conditions of all the workers," * continuing through the theory of stages, to the resolution of the congress on the "most widely applicable," etc., "economic struggle against the government" is precisely trade-union politics, which is far, far away from being Social-Democratic politics.

B. A Tale of How Martynov Rendered Plekhanov More Profound

"What a large number of Social-Democratic Lomonosovs ** appeared among us lately!" observed a comrade to me one day, having in mind the astonishing propensity of many of those who are inclined toward Economism to "seek for themselves" the great truths (for example, like the one that the economic struggle stimulates the workers to ponder over their lack of rights), and in doing so ignore, with the supreme contempt of born geniuses, all that which has already been produced by previous development of revolutionary thought and of the revolutionary movement. Precisely such a born genius is Lomonosov-Martynov. Glance at his article, "Immediate Questions," and observe how he "in his way" *approaches* that which has been said long ago by Axelrod (and whom our Lomonosov silently ignores); how, for example, he is *beginning* to understand that we must not ignore the opposition of the various strata of the bourgeoisie [*Rabocheye Dyelo* No. 9, pp. 61-62-71; compare this with *Rabocheye Dyelo's Reply* to Axelrod, pp. 22-23-24], etc. But alas, he is only "approaching" and is only "beginning," not more than that, for so little has he understood Axelrod's ideas, that he talks about "the economic struggle against the employers and the government." For three years (1898-1901) *Rabocheye Dyelo* has tried hard to understand Axelrod, but has failed to do so yet! Perhaps this is because Social-Democracy, "like humanity," always sets itself only tasks that can be achieved.

But the Lomonosovs are distinguished not only by the fact of their ignorance of many things (that would not be so bad!) but also by the fact that they are not conscious of their ignorance. Now this is a real misfortune, and this misfortune stimulates them to attempt to render Plekhanov "more profound."

* *Rabochaya Mysl*, Special Supplement, p. 14.
** Kholmogory Lomonosov (1711-1765), the inventive genius and the recognised father of Russian science.—*Ed.*

Lomonosov-Martynov writes:

Much water has flowed beneath the bridges since Plekhanov wrote this book. [*Socialist Tasks in the Fight against the Famine in Russia*]. The Social-Democrats who for a decade led the economic struggle of the working class . . . have failed as yet to lay down a broad theoretical basis for party tactics. This question has now come to the fore, and if we would wish to lay down such a theoretical basis we would certainly have to considerably deepen the principles of tactics that Plekhanov at one time developed. . . . We would now have to define the difference between propaganda and agitation differently from the way in which Plekhanov defined it. [Martynov had just previously quoted the words of Plekhanov: "A propagandist presents many ideas to one or a few persons; an agitator presents only one or a few ideas, but he presents them to a mass of people."] By propaganda we would understand the revolutionary elucidation of the whole of the present system or partial manifestations of it, irrespective of whether it is done in a form capable of being understood by individuals or by the broad masses. By agitation, in the strict sense of the word [*sic!*] we would understand: Calling the masses to certain concrete actions that would facilitate the direct revolutionary intervention of the proletariat in social life

We congratulate Russian, and international Social-Democracy on Martynov's more strict and more profound terminology. Up till now we thought (with Plekhanov, and with all the leaders of the international labour movement), that a propagandist, dealing with say the question of unemployment, must explain the capitalistic nature of crises, the reasons why crises are inevitable in modern society, must describe how present society must inevitably become transformed into Socialist society, etc. In a word, he must present "many ideas," so many indeed that they will be understood as a whole only by a (comparatively) few persons. An agitator, however, speaking on the same subject will take as an illustration a fact that is most widely known and outstanding among his audience —say the death from starvation of the family of an unemployed worker, the growing impoverishment, etc.—and utilising this illustration, will direct all his efforts to present *a single idea* to the "masses," *i. e.*, the idea of the senseless contradiction between the increase of wealth and increase of poverty; he will strive to *rouse* discontent and indignation among the masses against this crying injustice, and leave a more complete explanation of this contradiction to the propagandist. Consequently, the propagandist operates chiefly by means of the *printed* word; the agitator operates with the *living* word. The qualities that are required of an agitator are not the same as the qualities that are required of a propagandist. Kautsky and Lafargue, for example, we call propagandists; Bebel and Guesde we call agitators. To point to a third sphere, or third function, of practical activity, and to include in this third function "calling the masses to certain concrete actions," is sheer nonsense, because the "call," as a single act, either naturally and inevitably supplements the theoretical tract, propagandist pamphlet and agitational speech, or represents a purely executive function. Take, for example, the struggle now being carried on by the German Social-Democrats against the grain duties. The theoreticians write researches in tariff policy and "call" say, for a fight for commercial treaties and for free trade. The propagandist does the same thing in the periodical press, and the agitator does it in public speeches. At the present time, the "concrete action" of the masses takes the form of signing petitions to the Reichstag against the raising of the grain duties. The call for this action comes directly from the theoreticians, the propagandists and the agitators, and indirectly, from those workers who carry the petition lists to the factories and to private houses to get signatures. According to the "Martynov terminology," Kautsky and Bebel are both propagandists, while those who carry the petition lists around are agitators; is that not so?

The German example recalled to my mind the German word *Verballhornung*, which literally translated means "to Ballhorn." Johann Ballhorn, a Leipzig publisher of the sixteenth century, published a child's reader in which, as was the custom, he introduced a drawing of a cock; but this drawing, instead of portraying an ordinary cock with spurs, portrayed it without spurs and with a couple of eggs lying near it. On the cover of this reader he printed the legend *"Revised edition by Johann Ballhorn."* Since that time the Germans describe any "Revision" that is really a worsening, as "Ballhorning." And watching Martynov's attempts to render Plekhanov "more profound" involuntarily recalls Ballhorn to one's mind. . . .

Why did our Lomonosov "invent" this confusion? In order to illustrate how *Iskra* "devotes attention only to one side of the case, just as Plekhanov did a decade and a half ago" [p. 39]. "According to *Iskra*, propagandist tasks force agitational tasks into the background, at least for the present" [p. 52]. If we translate this last postulate from the language of Martynov into ordinary human language (because humanity has not yet managed to learn the newly invented terminology), we shall get the following: "According to *Iskra*, the tasks of political propaganda and political agitation force

66

into the background the task of 'presenting to the government concrete demands for legislative and administrative measures' that
promise certain palpable results" (or demands for social reforms,
that is if we are permitted just once again to employ the old terminology of old humanity, which has not yet grown to Martynov's
level). We suggest that the reader compare this thesis with the
following tirade:

> What astonishes us in these programmes [the programmes advanced by
> revolutionary Social-Democrats], is the constant stress that is laid upon the
> benefits of labour activity in parliament (non-existent in Russia) and the
> manner in which (thanks to their revolutionary Nihilism) the importance of
> workers participating in the Government Advisory Committees on Factory
> Affairs (which do exist in Russia) . . . or at least the importance of workers
> participating in municipal bodies, is completely ignored. . . .

The author of this tirade expresses more straightforwardly, more
clearly and frankly, the very idea which, although Lomonosov-
Martynov discovered it himself, actually originated in the mind of
R. M. in the Special Supplement of *Rabochaya Mysl* [p. 15].

C. POLITICAL EXPOSURES AND "TRAINING IN REVOLUTIONARY ACTIVITY"

In advancing against *Iskra* his "theory" of "raising the activity
of the masses of the workers," Martynov, as a matter of fact, displayed a striving to *diminish* this activity, because he declared the
very economic struggle before which all Economists grovel to be
the preferable, the most important and "the most widely applicable
means of rousing this activity, and the widest field for it." This
error is such a characteristic one, precisely because it is not peculiar
to Martynov alone. As a matter of fact, it is possible to "raise
the activity of the masses of the workers" *only* provided this activity
is not restricted entirely to "political agitation on an economic
basis." And one of the fundamental conditions for the necessary expansion of political agitation is the organisation of *all-sided* political
exposure. In *no other way* can the masses be trained in political
consciousness and revolutionary activity except by means of such
exposures. Hence, to conduct such activity is one of the most
important functions of international Social-Democracy as a whole,
for even in countries where political liberty exists, there is still
a field for work of exposure, although in such countries the work

is conducted in a different sphere. For example, the German party is strengthening its position and spreading its influence, thanks particularly to the untiring energy with which it is conducting a campaign of political exposure. Working-class consciousness cannot be genuinely political consciousness unless the workers are trained to respond to all cases of tyranny, oppression, violence and abuse, no matter *what class* is affected. Moreover, that response must be a Social-Democratic response, and not one from any other point-of-view. The consciousness of the masses of the workers cannot be genuine class consciousness, unless the workers learn to observe from concrete, and above all from topical, political facts and events, *every* other social class and *all* the manifestations of the intellectual, ethical and political life of these classes; unless they learn to apply practically the materialist analysis and the materialist estimate of *all* aspects of the life and activity of *all* classes, strata and groups of the population. Those who concentrate the attention, observation and the consciousness of the working class exclusively, or even mainly, upon itself alone, are not Social-Democrats; because, for its self-realisation the working class must not only have a theoretical . . . rather it would be more true to say: Not so much theoretical as a practical understanding acquired through experience of political life of the relationships between *all* classes of modern society. That is why the idea preached by our Economists, that the economic struggle is the most widely applicable means of drawing the masses into the political movement is so extremely harmful and extremely reactionary in practice. In order to become a Social-Democrat, a working man must have a clear picture in his mind of the economic nature and the social and political features of the landlord, of the priest, of the high state official and of the peasant, of the student and of the tramp; he must know their strong and weak sides; he must understand all the catch-words and sophisms by which each class and each stratum *camou-flages* its egotistical strivings and its real "nature"; he must understand what interests certain institutions and certain laws reflect and how they are reflected. The working man cannot obtain this "clear picture" from books. He can obtain it only from living examples and from exposures, following hot after their occurrence, of what goes on around us at a given moment, of what is being discussed, in whispers perhaps, by each one in his own way, of the meaning of such and such events, of such and such statistics, in such and such court sentences, etc., etc., etc. These universal political exposures are an essential and *fundamental* condition for training the masses in revolutionary activity.

Why is it that the Russian workers as yet display so little revolutionary activity in connection with the brutal way in which the police maltreat the people, in connection with the persecution of the religious sects, with the flogging of the peasantry, with the outrageous censorship, with the torture of soldiers, with the persecution of the most innocent cultural enterprises, etc.? Is it because the "economic struggle" does not "stimulate" them to this, because such political activity does not "promise palpable results," because it produces little that is "positive"? To advance this argument, we repeat, is merely to shift the blame to the shoulders of others, to blame the masses of the workers for our own philistinism (also Bernsteinism). We must blame ourselves, our remoteness from the mass movement; we must blame ourselves for being unable as yet to organise a sufficiently wide, striking and rapid exposure of these despicable outrages. When we do that (and we must and can do it), the most backward worker will understand, *or will feel,* that the students and religious sects, the muzhiks and the authors are being abused and outraged by the very same dark forces that are oppressing and crushing him at every step of his life, and, feeling that, he himself will be filled with an irresistible desire to respond to these things and then he will organise cat-calls against the censors one day, another day he will demonstrate outside the house of the provincial governor who has brutally suppressed peasant uprising, another day he will teach a lesson to the gendarmes in surplices who are doing the work of the Holy Inquisition, etc. As yet we have done very little, almost nothing, to *hurl* universal and fresh exposures among the masses of the workers. Many of us as yet do not appreciate the *bounden duty* that rests upon us, but spontaneously follow in the wake of the "drab every-day struggle," in the narrow confines of factory life. Under such circumstances to say that *Iskra* displays a tendency to belittle the significance of the forward march of the drab every-day struggle in comparison with the propaganda of brilliant and complete ideas [Martynov, p. 61]—means to drag the party backwards, to defend and glorify our unpreparedness and backwardness.

As for calling the masses to action, that will come of itself immediately that energetic political agitation, live and striking exposures are set going. To catch some criminal red-handed and immediately to brand him publicly will have far more effect than any number of "appeals to action"; the effect very often will be such, that it will be impossible to tell who exactly it was that "appealed" to the crowd, and who exactly suggested this or that plan of demonstration, etc. Calls for action, not in the general, but in the concrete, sense of the term, can be made only at the place of action; only those who themselves go into action now can make appeals for action. And our business as Social-Democratic publicists is to deepen, expand and intensify political exposures and political agitation. A word in passing about "calls to action." *The only paper* that *prior to* the spring events,* *called upon* the workers actively to intervene in a matter that certainly did *not promise* any *palpable results* for the workers, *i. e.*, the drafting of the students into the army, *was Iskra.* Immediately after the publication of the order of January 11 "Drafting the 183 Students into the Army," *Iskra* published an article about it (in its February issue, No. 2),** and *before* any demonstration was started openly *called upon* "the workers to go to the aid of the students," called upon the "people" boldly to take up the government's open challenge. We ask: How is the remarkable fact to be explained that although he talks so much about "calling for action," and even suggests "calling for action" as a special form of activity, Martynov said not a word about *this* call? After this, is not Martynov's allegation, that *Iskra* was *one-sided* because it did not sufficiently "call for" the struggle for demands "promising palpable results," sheer philistinism?

Our Economists, including *Rabocheye Dyelo*, were successful because they disguised themselves as uneducated workers. But the working-class Social-Democrat, the working-class revolutionist (and their number is growing) will indignantly reject all this talk about fighting for demands "promising palpable results," etc., because he will understand that this is only a variation of the old song about adding a kopeck to the ruble. These working-class revolutionaries will say to their counsellors of the *Rabochaya Mysl* and *Rabocheye Dyelo:* You are wasting your time, gentlemen; you are interfering with excessive zeal in a job that we can manage ourselves, and you are neglecting your own duties. It is silly of you to say that the

---

* This refers to the big street demonstrations which commenced in the spring of 1901.

** See *The Iskra Period*, Book I, p. 70.—*Ed.*

Social-Democrats's task is to give the economic struggle itself a political character, for that is only the beginning, it is not the main task that Social-Democrats must fulfil. All over the world, including Russia, *the police themselves often give* the economic struggle a political character, and the workers are beginning to understand whom the government supports.*

The "economic struggle between the workers and the employers and the government," about which you make as much fuss as if you had made a new discovery, is being carried on in all parts of Russia, even the most remote, by the workers themselves who have heard about strikes, but who have heard almost nothing about Socialism. The "activity" you want to stimulate among us workers by advancing concrete demands promising palpable results, we are already displaying and in our every-day, petty trade-union work, we put forward concrete demands, very often without any assistance from the intellectuals whatever. But *such* activity is not enough for us; we are not children to be fed on the sops of "economic" politics alone; we want to know everything that everybody else knows, we want to learn the details of *all* aspects of political life and to take part *actively* in every political event. In order that we may do this, the intellectuals must talk to us less on what we already know,** and tell us more about what we do not know and what we

* The demand "to give the economic struggle itself a political character" most strikingly expresses *subservience to spontaneity* in the sphere of political activity. Very often the economic struggle *spontaneously* assumes a political character, that is to say without the injection of the "revolutionary bacilli of the intelligentsia," without the intervention of the class-conscious Social-Democrats. For example, the economic struggle of the British workers assumed a political character without the intervention of the Socialists. The tasks of the Social-Democrats, however, are not exhausted by political agitation on the economic field; their task is to *convert* trade-union politics into the Social-Democratic political struggle, to *utilise* the flashes of political consciousness which gleam in the minds of the workers during their economic struggles for the purpose of *raising* them to the level of *Social-Democratic* political consciousness. The Martynovs, however, instead of raising and stimulating the spontaneously awakening political consciousness of the workers, *bow down before spontaneity* and repeat over and over again, until one is sick and tired of hearing it, that the economic struggle "stimulates" in the workers' minds thoughts about their own lack of political rights. It is unfortunate, gentlemen, that the spontaneously awakening trade-union political consciousness does not "*stimulate*" in your minds thoughts about your Social-Democratic tasks!

** To prove that this imaginary speech of a worker to an Economist is based on fact, we shall call two witnesses who undoubtedly have direct knowledge of the labour movement, and who can be at least suspected of being partial towards us "doctrinaires," for one witness is an Economist (who recan never learn from our factory and "economic" experience, that is, you must give us political knowledge. You intellectuals can acquire this knowledge, and it is your *duty* to bring us that knowledge in a hundred and a thousand times greater measure than you have done up till now; and you must bring us this knowledge, not only in the form of arguments, pamphlets and articles which some-times—excuse my frankness!—are very dull, but in the form of live *exposures* of what our government and our governing classes are doing at this very moment in all spheres of life. Fulfil this duty with greater zeal, and *talk less about "increasing the activity of the masses of the workers"!* We are far more active than you think, and we are quite able to support by open street fighting demands that do not even promise any "palpable results" whatever! You cannot "increase" our activity, because *you yourselves are not sufficiently active.* Be less subservient to spontaneity, and think more about increasing *your own* activity, gentlemen!

D. WHAT IS THERE IN COMMON BETWEEN ECONOMISM AND TERRORISM?

In the last footnote we quoted the opinion of an Economist and of a non-Social-Democratic terrorist who, by chance, proved to be in agreement with him. Speaking generally, however, between the two there is not an accidental, but a necessary mutual connection,

gards even *Rabocheye Dyelo* as a political organ!), and the other is a terrorist. The first witness is the author of a remarkably truthful and lively article entitled "The St. Petersburg Labour Movement and the Practical Tasks of Social-Democracy," published in *Rabocheye Dyelo*, No. 6. He divided the workers into the following categories: 1. Conscious revolutionaries; 2. Intermediate stratum; and 3. The Masses. Now the intermediate stratum he says "is often more interested in questions of political life than in its own immediate economic interests, the connection between which and the general social conditions it has long understood. . . ." *Rabochaya Mysl* "is sharply criticised. It keeps on repeating the same thing over and over again, things we have long known, read long ago." "Nothing in the political review again!" [pp. 30-31]. But even the third stratum—the younger and more sensitive section of the workers, less corrupted by the vodka shop and the church, that has hardly ever had the opportunity of reading political literature, in a rambling way discuss political events and ponder deeply over the fragmentary news they get about the student riots, etc. The second witness, the terrorist, writes as follows: ". . . They read over once or twice the petty details of factory life in other towns, not their own, and then they read no more. . . . 'Awfully dull,' they say. . . . To say nothing in a workers' paper about the government . . . signifies that the workers are regarded as being little children. . . . The workers are not babies." [*Svoboda*, published by the Revolutionary Socialist group, pp. 67-70.]

about which we shall have to speak farther on in connection with the question of training the masses in revolutionary activity. The Economists and the modern terrorists spring from a common root, namely, *subservience to spontaneity*, which we dealt with in a previous chapter as a general phenomenon, and which we shall now examine in relation to its effect upon political activity and the political struggle. At first sight, our assertion may appear paradoxical, for the difference between these two appears to be so enormous: One stresses the "drab every-day struggle" and the other calls for the most self-sacrificing struggle of individuals. But this is not a paradox. The Economists and terrorists merely bow to different poles of spontaneity: The Economists bow to the spontaneity of the "pure and simple" labour movement while the terrorists bow to the spontaneity of the passionate indignation of the intellectuals, who are either incapable of linking up the revolutionary struggle with the labour movement, or lack the opportunity to do so. It is very difficult indeed for those who have lost their belief, or who have never believed, that this was possible, to find some other outlet for their indignation and revolutionary energy than terror. Thus, both the forms of subservience to spontaneity we have mentioned are nothing more nor less than *a beginning in the carrying out* of the notorious *Credo* programme. Let the workers carry on their "economic struggle against the employers and the government" (we apologise to the author of *Credo* for expressing his views in Martynov's words! But we think we have the right to do so because even the *Credo* says that in the economic struggle the workers "come up against the political régime"), and let the intellectuals conduct the political struggle by their own efforts—with the aid of terror, of course! This is an absolutely logical and inevitable *conclusion* which must be insisted upon—even though those who are beginning to carry out this programme did not themselves realise that it is inevitable. Political activity has its logic quite apart from the consciousness of those who, with the best intentions, call either for terror, or for giving the economic struggle itself a political character. The road to hell is paved with good intentions, and, in this case, good intentions cannot save one from being spontaneously drawn "along the line of least resistance," along the line of the *purely bourgeois Credo* programme. Surely it is not an accident that many Russian liberals—avowed liberals and liberals who wear the mask of Marxism—wholeheartedly sympathise with terror, and strive to foster the spirit of terrorism that is running so high at the present time.

The formation of the *Svoboda* Revolutionary Socialist group— which was formed with the object of giving all possible assistance to the labour movement, but which included in its *programme* terror, and emancipation, so to speak, from Social-Democracy—this fact once again confirmed the remarkable penetration of P. B. Axelrod who *literally foretold* these results of Social-Democratic wavering *as far back as* the end of 1897 [*Modern Tasks and Modern Tactics*], when he outlined his remarkable "two prospects." All the subsequent disputes and disagreements among Russian Social-Democrats are contained, like a plant in the seed, in these two prospects.*

From this point of view it will be clear that *Rabocheye Dyelo*, being unable to withstand the spontaneity of Economism, has been unable also to withstand the spontaneity of terrorism. It would be interesting to note here the specific arguments that *Svoboda* advanced in defence of terrorism. It "completely denies" the deterrent rôle of terrorism [*The Regeneration of Revolutionism*, p. 64], but instead stresses its "excitative significance." This is characteristic, firstly, as representing one of the stages of the break-up and decay of the traditional (pre-Social-Democratic) cycle of ideas which insisted upon terrorism. To admit now that the government cannot be "terrified," and therefore disrupted, by terror, is tantamount to condemning terror as a system of struggle, as a sphere of activity sanctioned by the programme. Secondly, it is still more characteristic as an example of the failure to understand our immediate task of "training

* Martynov "conceives of another, more realistic [?] dilemma" [*Social-Democracy and the Working Class*, p. 19]: "Either Social-Democracy undertakes the direct leadership of the economic struggle of the proletariat and by that [!] transforms it into a revolutionary class struggle . . ." "and by that," *i. e.*, apparently the direct leadership of the economic struggle. Can Martynov quote an example where the leadership of the industrial struggle *alone* has succeeded in transforming the trade-union movement into a revolutionary class movement? Cannot he understand that in order to "transform" we must undertake the "direct leadership" *of all-sided* political agitation? ". . . Or the other prospect: Social-Democracy refrains from taking the leadership of the economic struggle of the workers and so . . . clips its own wings. . . ." In *Rabocheye Dyelo's* opinion, which we quoted above, *Iskra* "refrains." We have seen, however, that the latter *does far more* to lead the economic struggle than *Rabocheye Dyelo*, but it does not confine itself to this, and does not *curtail* its political tasks for the sake of it.

; he must be able to tal
to explain his Socialist
mands *to all*, in order
historical significance o
roletariat.

Robert Knight (the cele
Makers Society, one of th
with Wilhelm Liebknecht
draws in his controversy
ing through Martynov's
in "calling the masses to
bknecht engaged more in
le of modern society, or
39]; that Robert Knight
e proletariat and pointed
ieved" [p. 41], whereas
multaneously guided the
ctated to them a positive
t was precisely Robert
ve to the economic strug-
was excellently able "to
s promising certain pal-
engaged more in "one-
Knight attached more
rab, every-day struggle"
in the "propaganda of
Liebknecht converted the
revolutionary opposition
rly the political condi-
rests of the most varied
Robert Knight "worked
tact with the proletarian
c contact" is meant the
udied above from the
d "restricted the sphere
is Martynov, that "by
In a word, you will see

Liebknecht dictated a pro-
and this was done to an

the masses in revolutionary activity." *Svoboda* advocates terror as a means of "exciting" the labour movement, and of giving it a "strong impetus." It is difficult to imagine an argument that disproves itself more than this one does! Are there not enough outrages committed in Russian life that a special "stimulant" has to be invented? On the other hand, is it not obvious that those who are not, and cannot be, roused to excitement even by Russian tyranny will stand by "twiddling their thumbs" even while a handful of terrorists are engaged in single combat with the government? The fact is, however, that the masses of the workers are roused to a high pitch of excitement by the outrages committed in Russian life, but we are unable to collect, if one may put it that way, and concentrate all these drops and streamlets of popular excitement that are called forth by the conditions of Russian life to a far larger extent than we imagine, but which it is precisely necessary to combine into a *single* gigantic flood. And this we must do. That this task can be accomplished is irrefutably proved by the enormous growth of the labour movement, and the greed with which the workers devour political literature, to which we have already referred above. Calls for terror, and calls to give the economic struggle itself a political character are merely two different forms of *evading* the most pressing duty that now rests upon Russian revolutionaries, namely, to organise an all-sided political agitation. *Svoboda* desires to *substitute* terror for agitation, although it openly admits that "as soon as intensified and strenuous agitation is commenced among the masses its excitative function will be finished." [*The Regeneration of Revolutionism*, p. 68.] This proves precisely that both the terrorists and the Economists *underestimate* the revolutionary activity of the masses, in spite of the striking evidence of the events that took place in the spring, and whereas one goes out in search of artificial "stimulants" the other talks about "concrete demands." But both fail to devote sufficient attention to the development *of their own activity* in political agitation and organisation of political exposures. And no other work can serve as a *substitute* for this work, either at the present time, or at any other time.

E. THE WORKING CLASS AS CHAMPION OF DEMOCRACY

We have seen that the organisation of wide political agitation, and consequently, of all-sided political exposures are an absolutely necessary *and paramount* task of activity, that is, if that activity is

to be truly Social-Democratic. We arrived at this co
on the grounds of the pressing needs of the working
cal knowledge and political training. But this gr
is too narrow for the presentation of the question,
the general democratic tasks of Social-Democracy a
of modern, Russian Social-Democracy in particular
explain the situation more concretely we shall appro
from an aspect that is "nearer" to the Economist, na
practical aspect. "Every one agrees" that it is necess
the political consciousness of the working class. Bu
arises, How is that to be done? What must be don
about? The economic struggle merely brings the
against" questions concerning the attitude of the gover
the working class. Consequently, *however much we m*
to the economic struggle itself a political character"
be able to develop the political consciousness of the w
degree of Social-Democratic consciousness) by confi
to the economic struggle, for *the limits of this task ar*
The Martynov formula has some value for us, not be
trates Martynov's abilities to confuse things, but be
ingly expresses the fundamental error that all the Ec
mit, namely, their conviction that it is possible to dev
political consciousness of the workers *from within*, t
exclusively, or at least mainly, by means of the econo
Such a view is radically wrong. Piqued by our oppos
the Economists refuse to ponder deeply over the ori
disagreements, with the result that we absolutely fail
each other. It is as if we spoke in different tongues.

The workers can acquire class political consciousne
without, that is, only outside of the economic struggle,
sphere of relations between workers and employers.
from which alone it is possible to obtain this know
sphere of relationships between *all* classes and the
government—the sphere of the inter-relations betweer
For that reason, the reply to the question: What mus
order that the workers may acquire political knowledg
merely the one which, in the majority of cases, the pract
especially those who are inclined towards Econom
content themselves with, *i. e.*, "go among the workers.

76

police violence and capitalist exploitatio
advantage of every petty event in order
convictions and his Social-Democratic d
explain to *all* and every one the worl
the struggle for the emancipation of the

Compare, for example, a leader like
brated secretary and leader of the Boiler
most powerful trade unions in England)
and then take the contrasts that Martyno
with *Iskra*. You will see—I am run
article—that Robert Knight engaged mor
certain concrete actions" [p. 39] while Li
"the revolutionary explanation of the wh
various manifestations of it" [pp. 38–
"formulated the immediate demands of th
to the manner in which they can be ac
Wilhelm Liebknecht, while doing this "s
activities of various opposition strata," "d
programme of action" [p. 41]; * that
Knight who strove "as far as possible to g
gle itself a political character" [p. 42] an
submit to the government concrete deman
pable results" [p. 43], while Liebknecht
sided exposures" [p. 40]; that Rober
significance to the "forward march of the
[p. 61], while Liebknecht engaged more
brilliant and finished ideas" [p. 61]; that
paper he was directing into "an organ of
exposing the present system and particul
tions which came into conflict with the int
strata of the population" [p. 63], whereas
for the cause of labour in close organic co
struggle" [p. 63]—if by "close and organ
subservience to spontaneity which we s
example of Krichevsky and Martynov—an
of his influence," convinced, of course, a
that he intensified that influence" [p. 63].

* For example, during the Franco-Prussian War
gramme of action *for the whole of democracy*—
even greater extent by Marx and Engels in 1848.
78

that *de facto*, Martynov reduces Social-Democracy to the level of trade unionism, and he does this, of course, not because he does not desire the good of Social-Democracy, but simply because he was a little too much in a hurry to make Plekhanov more profound, instead of taking the trouble to understand him.

Let us return, however, to the elucidation of our thesis. We said that a Social-Democrat, if he really believes it is necessary to develop the political consciousness of the proletariat, must "go among all classes of the people." This gives rise to the questions: How is this to be done? Have we enough forces to do this? Is there a base for such work among all the other classes? Will this not mean a retreat, or lead to a retreat from the class point-of-view? We shall deal with these questions.

We must "go among all classes of the people" as theoreticians, as propagandists, as agitators, and as organisers. No one doubts that the theoretical work of Social-Democrats should be directed towards studying all the features of the social and political position of the various classes. But extremely little is done in this direction compared with the work that is done in studying the features of factory life. In the committees and circles, you will meet men who are immersed say in the study of some special branch of the metal industry, but you will hardly ever find members of organisations (obliged, as often happens, for some reason or other to give up practical work) especially engaged in the collection of material concerning some pressing question of social and political life which could serve as a means for conducting Social-Democratic work among other strata of the population. In speaking of the lack of training of the majority of present-day leaders of the labour movement, we cannot refrain from mentioning the point about training in this connection also, for it is also bound up with the "economic" conception of "close organic contact with the proletarian struggle." The principal thing, of course, is *propaganda and agitation* among all strata of the people. The Western-European Social-Democrats find their work in this field facilitated by the calling of public meetings, to which *all* are free to go, and by the parliament, in which they speak to the representatives of *all* classes. We have neither a parliament, nor the freedom to call meetings, nevertheless we are able to arrange meetings of workers who desire to listen to *a Social-Democrat*. We must also find ways and means of calling meetings of representatives of all and every other class of the population that desire to listen to a *Democrat;* for he who forgets that "the Communists support every revolutionary movement," that we are obliged for that reason to emphasize *general democratic tasks before the whole people,* without for a moment concealing our Socialistic convictions, is not a Social-Democrat. He who forgets his obligation to *be in advance of everybody* in bringing up, sharpening and solving *every* general democratic question, is not a Social-Democrat.

"But everybody agrees with this!"—the impatient reader will exclaim—and the new instructions given by the last congress of the League to the Editorial Board of *Rabocheye Dyelo* says: "All events of social and political life that affect the proletariat either directly as a special class or *as the vanguard of all the revolutionary forces in the struggle for freedom* should serve as subjects for political propaganda and agitation." [*Two Congresses,* p. 17, our italics.]

Yes, these are very true and very good words and we would be satisfied if *Rabocheye Dyelo understood them, and if it refrained from saying in the next breath things that are the very opposite to them.* Surely, it is not sufficient to call ourselves the "vanguard," it is necessary to act like one; we must act in such a way that all the other units of the army shall see us, and be obliged to admit that we are the vanguard. And we ask the reader: Are the representatives of the other "units" such fools as to take merely our word for it when we say that we are the "vanguard"?

Just picture to yourselves the following: A Social-Democrat comes into the "unit" of Russian educated radicals, or liberal constitutionalists, and declares to them: We are the vanguard; "at the present time we are confronted by the problem of—how to give as far as possible to the economic struggle itself a political character." The radical, or constitutionalist, if he is at all intelligent (and there are many intelligent men among Russian radicals and constitutionalists), would only laugh at such a speech, and would say (to himself, of course, for in the majority of cases they are experienced diplomats):

Well, your "vanguard" must be composed of simpletons! It does not even understand that it is our task, the task of the progressive representatives of bourgeois democracy to give to the economic struggle of the workers a political character. Why, we too, like all the West-European bourgeoisie, are striving to draw the workers into politics, but *only into trade-union politics and not into Social-Democratic politics.* Trade-union politics are precisely *bourgeois politics* of the working class and the "vanguard's" formulation of its tasks is the formula for trade-union politics. Let them call themselves "Social-Democrats if they like, I am not a child to get excited over a label. But see that they do not fall under tthe influence of those pernicious orthodox doctrinaires, let them allow "freedom of criticism" to those who unconsciously are driving Social-Democracy into trade-unionist channels.

And the light chuckle of our constitutionalist will turn into Homeric laughter when he learns that the Social-Democrats who talk about Social-Democracy being the vanguard at the present time, when spontaneity completely dominates our movement, fears nothing so much as "belittling the spontaneous elements," as "belittling the significance of the forward march of the drab, every-day struggle, as compared with the propaganda of brilliant and finished ideas," etc., etc.! A "vanguard," which fears that consciousness will outstrip spontaneity, which fears to put forward a bold "plan" that would compel universal recognition even among those who think differently from us—Are they not confusing the word "vanguard" with the word "rearguard"?

Ponder over the following piece of Martynov reasoning. On page 42 he says that *Iskra's* tactics of exposing abuses are one-sided, that "however much we may spread distrust and hatred towards the government, we shall not achieve our aim until we have succeeded in developing sufficiently active social energy for its overthrow." This, it may be said in parenthesis, is the concern we have already met with for increasing the activity of the masses, while at the same time striving to restrict its activity. This is not the point we are now discussing, however. Martynov, therefore, speaks of *revolutionary* energy ("for its overthrow"). But what conclusion does he arrive at? As in ordinary times, various social strata inevitably march separately, therefore,

> In view of that, it is clear that we Social-Democrats cannot simultaneously guide the activities of various opposition strata, we cannot dictate to them a positive programme of action, we cannot point out to them in what manner they can fight for their daily interests. . . . The liberal strata will themselves take care of the active struggle for their immediate interests and this struggle will bring them up against our political régime.

Thus, having commenced by speaking about revolutionary energy —of the active struggle for the overthrow of the autocracy, Martynov immediately turned towards trade-union energy and active struggle for immediate interests! It goes without saying that we cannot guide the struggle of the students, liberals, etc., for their "immediate interests," but this is not the point we were arguing about, most worthy Economists! The point we were discussing is the possible and necessary participation of various social strata in the overthrow of the autocracy; not only are we able, but it is our duty to guide *these* "activities, of the various opposition strata" if we desire to be a "vanguard." Not only will the students and our liberals, etc., take care of the struggle that will bring them up against our political régime; the police and the officials of the auto-cratic government will see to this more than any one. But, if "we" desire to be advanced democrats, we must make it our business to *stimulate* in the minds of those who are dissatisfied only with university or only with Zemstvo, etc., conditions the idea that the whole political system is worthless. We must take upon ourselves the task of organising a universal political struggle under the lead-ership of *our party* in such a manner as to obtain the support of all opposition strata for the struggle and for our party. We must train our Social-Democratic practical workers to become political leaders, able to guide all the manifestations of this universal struggle, able at the right time to "dictate a positive programme of action" for the discontented students, for the discontented Zemstvo, for the discontented religious sects, for the offended elementary school teachers, etc., etc. For that reason, Martynov's assertion that "with regard to these, we can come forward merely in *the negative* rôle of exposers of abuses . . . we can *only* dissipate the hopes they have in various government commissions"—*is absolutely wrong* (our italics). By saying this Martynov shows that *he abso-lutely fails to understand* the rôle the revolutionary "vanguard" must really play. If the reader bears this in mind, the *real sense* of the following concluding remarks by Martynov will be clear to him:

Iskra is the organ of the revolutionary opposition which exposes the abuses of our system—particularly political abuses, in so far as they affect the interests of the most diverse classes of the population. We, however, are working and will continue to work for the cause of labour in close organic contact with the proletarian struggle. By restricting the sphere of our in-fluence, we at the same time intensify that influence.

The true sense of this conclusion is as follows: *Iskra* desires to elevate working-class trade-union politics (to which, owing to mis-understanding, lack of training, or by conviction our practical work-ers frequently confine themselves) to Social-Democratic politics, whereas *Rabocheye Dyelo* desires to *degrade* Social-Democratic poli-tics to trade-union politics. And while doing this, they assure the world that these two positions are "quite compatible in the common cause." *O! sancta simplicitas!*

To proceed. Have we sufficient forces to be able to direct our propaganda and agitation among *all* classes of the population? Of course we have. Our Economists are frequently inclined to deny this. They lose sight of the gigantic progress our movement has made from (approximately) 1894 to 1901. Like real Khvostists, they frequently live in the distant past, in the period of the beginning of the movement. At that time, indeed, we had astonishingly few forces, and it was perfectly natural and legitimate then to resolve to go exclusively among the workers, and severely condemn any deviation from this. The whole task then was to consolidate our position in the working class. At the present time, however, gigantic forces have been attracted to the movement; the best representatives of the young generation of the educated classes are coming over to us; everywhere, and in all provinces, there are people who have taken part in the movement in the past, who desire to do so now, who are striving towards Social-Democracy, but who are obliged to sit idle because we cannot employ them (in 1894 you could count the Social-Democrats on your fingers). One of the principal political and organisational shortcomings of our movement is that we are *unable* to utilise all these forces, and give them appropriate work (we shall deal with this in detail in the next chapter). The overwhelming majority of these forces entirely lack the opportunity for "going to the workers," so there are no grounds for fearing that we shall deflect forces from our main cause. And in order to be able to provide the workers with real, universal, and live political knowledge, we must have "our own men," Social-Democrats, everywhere, among all social strata, and in all positions from which we can learn the inner springs of our state mechanism. Such men are required for propaganda and agitation, but in a still larger measure for organisation.

Is there scope for activity among all classes of the population? Those who fail to see this also lag intellectually behind the spontaneous awakening of the masses. The labour movement has aroused and is continuing to arouse discontent in some, hopes for support for the opposition in others, and the consciousness of the intolerableness and inevitable downfall of autocracy in still others. We would be "politicians" and Social-Democrats only in name (as very often happens), if we failed to realise that our task is to

83

utilise every manifestation of discontent, and to collect and utilise every grain of even rudimentary protest. This is quite apart from the fact that many millions of the peasantry, handicraftsmen, petty artisans, etc., always listen eagerly to the preachings of any Social-Democrat who is at all intelligent. Is there a single class of the population in which no individuals, groups or circles are to be found who are discontented with the state of tyranny, and therefore accessible to the propaganda of Social-Democrats as the spokesmen of the most pressing general democratic needs? To those who desire to have a clear idea of what the political agitation of a Social-Democrat *among all* classes and strata of the population should be like, we would point to *political exposures* in the broad sense of the word as the principal (but of course not the sole) form of this agitation.

We must "arouse in every section of the population that is at all enlightened a passion for *political* exposure," I wrote in my article "Where to Begin" (*Iskra*, No. 4, May, 1901), with which I shall deal in greater detail later.

"We must not allow ourselves to be discouraged by the fact that the voice of political exposure is still feeble, rare and timid. This is not because of a general submission to political despotism, but because those who are able and ready to expose have no tribune from which to speak, because there is no audience to listen eagerly to and approve of what the orators say, and because the latter can nowhere perceive among the people forces to whom it would be worth while directing their complaint against the 'omnipotent' Russian government. . . . We are now in a position to set up a tribune for the national exposure of the tsarist government, and it is our duty to do so. That tribune must be a Social-Democratic paper. . . ." *

The ideal audience for these political exposures is the working class, which is first and foremost in need of universal and live political knowledge, which is most capable of converting this knowledge into active struggle, even if it did not promise "palpable results." The only platform from which *public* exposures can be made is an All-Russian newspaper. "Unless we have a political organ, a movement deserving the name of political is inconceivable in modern Europe." In this connection Russia must undoubtedly be included in modern Europe. The press has long ago become a power in our country, otherwise the government would not spend tens of thousands of rubles to bribe it, and to subsidise the Katkovs, and Meshcherskys. And it is no novelty in autocratic Russia for the underground press to break through the wall of censorship and

* See *The Iskra Period*, Book I, p. 113.—*Ed.*

compel the legal and conservative press to speak openly of it. This was the case in the seventies and even in the fifties. How much broader and deeper are now the strata of the people willing to read the illegal underground press, and to learn from it "how to live and how to die," to use the expression of the worker who sent a letter to *Iskra* [No. 7]. Political exposures are as much a declaration of war against the *government* as economic exposures are a declaration of war against the employers. And the wider and more powerful this campaign of exposure will be, the more numerous and determined the social *class* which has *declared war in order to commence the war* will be, the greater will be the moral significance of this declaration of war. Hence, political exposures in themselves serve as a powerful instrument for *disintegrating* the system we oppose, the means for diverting from the enemy his casual or temporary allies, the means for spreading enmity and distrust among those who permanently share power with the autocracy.

Only a party that will *organise* real all-national exposures can become the vanguard of the revolutionary forces in our time. The word "all-national" has a very profound meaning. The overwhelming majority of the non-working class exposers (and in order to become the vanguard, we must attract other classes) are sober politicians and cool business men. They know perfectly well how dangerous it is to "complain" even against a minor official, let alone against the "omnipotent" Russian government. And they will come *to us* with their complaints only when they see that these complaints really have effect, and when they see that we represent a *political* force. In order to become this political force in the eyes of outsiders, much persistent and stubborn work is required to *increase* our own consciousness, initiative and energy. For this, it is not sufficient to stick the label "vanguard" on "rearguard" theory and practice.

But if we have to undertake the organisation of the real all-national exposure of the government, then in what way will the class character of our movement be expressed?—the over-zealous advocates of "close organic contact with the proletarian struggle" will ask us. The reply is: In that we *Social-Democrats* will *organise* these public exposures; in that all the questions that are brought up by the agitation will be explained in the spirit of Social-Democracy, without any deliberate or unconscious distortions of Marxism; in the fact that *the party* will carry on this universal political agitation, uniting into one inseparable whole the pressure upon the government in the name of the whole people, the revolutionary training of the proletariat—while preserving its political independence—the guidance of the economic struggle of the working class, the utilisation of all its spontaneous conflicts with its exploiters, which rouse and bring into our camp increasing numbers of the proletariat!

But one of the characteristic features of Economism is its failure to understand this connection. More than that—it fails to understand the identity between the most pressing needs of the proletariat (an all-sided political education through the medium of political agitation and political exposures), and the need for a general democratic movement. This lack of understanding is not only expressed in "Martynovist" phrases, but also in the alleged class point-of-view which is identical in thought with these phrases. The following, for example, is how the authors of the Economic Letter in No. 12 of *Iskra* expressed themselves.*

This fundamental drawback [overestimating ideology] is the cause of *Iskra's* inconsistency in regard to the question of the relations between Social-Democrats and various social classes and tendencies. By a process of theoretical reasoning [and not by "the growth of party tasks which grow together with the party"], *Iskra* arrived at the conclusion that it was necessary immediately to take up the struggle against absolutism, but in all probability sensing the difficulty of this task for the workers in the present state of affairs [not only sensing, but knowing perfectly well that this problem will seem less difficult to the workers than to those Economist intellectuals who are concerned about little children, for the workers are prepared to fight even for demands which, to use the language of the never-to-be-forgotten Martynov, do not "promise palpable results"] and lacking the patience to wait until the working class has accumulated sufficient forces for this struggle, *Iskra* begins to seek for allies in the ranks of the liberals and intellectuals.

Yes, yes, we have indeed lost all "patience" to "wait" for the blessed time that has long been promised us by the "conciliators," when the Economists will stop throwing the blame for their *own* backwardness upon the workers, and stop justifying their own lack of energy by the alleged lack of energy of the workers. We ask our Economists: What does "the workers accumulating forces for the

* Lack of space has prevented us from replying in full to this letter extremely characteristic of the Economists. We were very glad this letter appeared, for the charges brought against *Iskra*, that it did not maintain a consistent, class point-of-view, have reached us long ago from various sources, and we waited for an appropriate opportunity, or for a formulated expression of this fashionable charge, in order to reply to it. And it is our habit to reply to attacks, not by defence, but by counter-attacks.

struggle" mean? Is it not evident that it means the political training of the workers by revealing to them *all* the aspects of our despicable autocracy? And is it not clear that *precisely for this work* we need "allies in the ranks of the liberals and intelligentsia," who are prepared to join us in the exposure of the political attack on the Zemstvo, on the teachers, on the statisticians, on the students, etc.? Is this "cunning mechanism" so difficult to understand after all? Did not P. B. Axelrod repeat to you over and over again since 1897: "The problem of the Russian Social-Democrats acquiring direct and indirect allies from among the non-proletarian classes will be solved principally by the character of the propagandist activities conducted among the proletariat itself?" And Martynov and the other Economists continue to image that the workers must *at first* accumulate forces (for trade-union politics) in the economic struggle with the employers and the government, and *then* "go over [we suppose from trade-union "training for activity"] to Social-Democratic activity."

. . . In its quest, continue the Economists, *Iskra* "not infrequently departs from the class point-of-view, obscures class antagonisms and puts into the forefront the general discontent prevailing against the government, notwithstanding the fact that the causes and the degree of his discontent vary very considerably among the 'allies.' Such, for example, is *Iskra's* attitude towards the Zemstvo. . . ."

Iskra, it is alleged, promises those who are discontented with the government's doles to the nobility the aid of the working class, but does not say a word about the class differences among these strata of the people. If the reader will turn to the series of articles "The Autocracy and the Zemstvo" [Nos. 2 and 4 of *Iskra*] to which, *in all probability*, the author of the letter refers, he will find that these articles * deal with the attitude of the *government* towards the "mild agitation of the feudal-bureaucratic Zemstvo," and towards the "independent activity of even the propertied classes." In these articles it is stated that the workers cannot look on indifferently while the government is carrying on a fight against the Zemstvo, and the latter are called upon to give up making soft speeches, but to speak firmly and resolutely when revolutionary Social-Democracy confronts the government in all its strength. What there is in this that

---

* *Among* these articles there was one (*Iskra*, No. 3) especially dealing with the class antagonisms in rural districts. [See *The Iskra Period*, Book I, p. 101.—*Ed.*]

the authors of the letter do not agree with is not clear. Do they think that the workers will "not understand" the phrases "propertied classes" and "feudal-bureaucratic Zemstvo"? Do they think that *stimulating* the Zemstvo to abandon soft speeches and to speak firmly and resolutely is "over-estimating ideology"? Do they imagine that the workers can accumulate "forces" for the fight against absolutism if they know nothing about the attitude of absolutism towards the Zemstvo? All this remains unknown. One thing alone is clear and that is that the authors of the letter have a very vague idea of what the political tasks of Social-Democracy are. This is revealed still more clearly by their remark: "Such also is *Iskra's* attitude towards the student movements" (*i. e.*, also "obscures class antagonism"). Instead of calling upon the workers to declare by means of public demonstrations that the real centre of unbridled violence and outrage is not the students but the Russian government [*Iskra,* No. 2],* we ought, no doubt, to have inserted arguments in the spirit of *Rabochaya Mysl.* And such ideas were expressed by Social-Democrats in the autumn of 1901, after the events of February and March, on the eve of a fresh student up-grade movement, which revealed that even in this sphere the "spontaneous" protest against autocracy is *"outstripping"* the conscious Social-Democratic leadership of the movement. The spontaneous striving of the workers to defend the students, who were being beaten up by the police and the Cossacks, is outstripping the conscious activity of the Social-Democratic organisations!

"And yet in other articles," continue the authors of the letter, *"Iskra* 'condemns' all 'compromises,' and 'defends,' for example, the intolerant conduct of the Guesdists." We would advise those who so conceitedly and frivolously declare—usually in connection with the disagreements existing among the contemporary Social-Democrats—that the disagreements are not essential and would not justify a split, to ponder very deeply over these words. Is it possible for those who say that we have done astonishingly little to explain the hostility of the autocracy towards the various classes, and to inform the workers of the opposition of the various strata of the population towards autocracy, to work successfully in one organisation with those who say that such work is "compromise"—evidently compromise with the theory of the "economic struggle against the employers and the government"?

* See *The Iskra Period*, Book I, p. 70.—*Ed.*

We urged the necessity of introducing the class struggle in the rural districts on the occasion of the fortieth anniversary of the emancipation of the peasantry (No. 3,* and of the irreconcilability between the local government bodies and the autocracy in connection with Witte's secret memorandum (No. 4). We attacked the feudal landlords and the government which served the latter on the occasion of the passing of the law (No. 8),** and welcomed the secret Zemstvo congress that was held. We urged the Zemstvo to stop making degrading petitions [No. 8], and to come out in the open to fight. We encouraged the students, who began to understand the necessity for the political struggle and began to take up that struggle [No. 3], and at the same time, we lashed out at the "barbarous lack of understanding" revealed by the adherents of the "purely student" movement, who called upon the students to abstain from taking part in the street demonstrations (No. 3, in connection with the manifesto issued by the Executive Committee of the Moscow students on February 25). We exposed the "senseless dreams" and the "lying hypocrisy" of the cunning liberals of *Rossiya* [No. 5] and at the same time we commented on the savage acts of the government's torture chambers where "peaceful writers, aged professors, and scientists and the liberal Zemstvo were cruelly dealt with" [No. 5, "The Police Raid on Literature"]. We exposed the real significance of the programme of the "concern of the government for the welfare of the workers," and welcomed the "valuable admission" that "it is better by granting reforms from above to forestall the demand for such reforms from below, than to wait for those demands to be put forward" [No. 6].*** We encouraged the protests of the statisticians [No. 7], and censured the strikebreaking statisticians [No. 9]. He who sees in these tactics the obscuring of the class consciousness of the proletariat and *compromise with liberalism* shows that he absolutely fails to understand the true significance of the programme of the *Credo* and *de facto is carrying out that programme*, however much he may deny this! Because, by that he is dragging Social-Democracy towards the "economic struggle against the employers and the government" but *shies at liberalism,* aban-

* See *The Iskra Period*, Book I, p. 101.—*Ed.*
** See *Ibid.*, p. 176.—*Ed.*
*** See *Ibid.*, p. 164.—*Ed.*

dons the task of actively intervening *in every* "liberal" question and defining *his own* Social-Democratic attitude towards such questions.

F. Again "Slanderers," Again "Mystifiers"

As the reader will remember, these polite expressions were uttered by *Rabocheye Dyelo* * which in this way answers our charge that it "indirectly prepared the ground for converting the labour movement into an instrument of bourgeois democracy." In its simplicity of heart *Rabocheye Dyelo* decided that this accusation was nothing more than a polemical sally, as if to say, these malicious doctrinaires can only think of saying unpleasant things about us; now what can be more unpleasant than being an instrument of bourgeois democracy? And so they print in heavy type a "refutation": "Nothing but downright slander" [*Two Congresses*, p. 30], "mystification" [p. 31] "masquerade" [p. 33]. Like Jupiter, *Rabocheye Dyelo* (although it has little resemblance to Jupiter) is angry because it is wrong, and proves by its hasty abuse that it is incapable of understanding its opponents' mode of reasoning. And yet, with only a little reflection, it would have understood why subservience to the spontaneity of the mass movement and any degrading of Social-Democratic politics to trade-union politics mean precisely to prepare the ground for converting the labour movement into an instrument of bourgeois democracy. The spontaneous labour movement is able by itself to create (and inevitably will create) only trade unionism, and working-class trade-union politics are precisely working-class bourgeois politics. The fact that the working class participates in the political struggle and even in political revolution does not in itself make its politics Social-Democratic politics. Will *Rabocheye Dyelo* deny that? Will it at last openly and without equivocation explain its position on the urgent questions of the international and of the Russian Social-Democratic movement? Oh no, it never thinks of doing anything of the kind, because it holds fast to the trick, which might be described as telling it in "negatives": "It's not me; it's not my horse; I'm not the driver." ** We are not Economists; *Rabochaya Mysl* does not stand for Economism; there is no Economism at all

---

* See *The Iskra Period*, Book I, p. 164.—*Ed.*

** A popular version of the excuses offered by a gipsy caught with a stolen horse.—*Ed.*

in Russia. This is a remarkably adroit and "political" trick, which suffers from this little defect, however, that the bodies that practice it are usually dubbed with the nickname: "Anything you wish, sir." *

Rabocheye Dyelo imagines that bourgeois democracy in Russia is merely a "phantom" [*Two Congresses*, p. 32].** Happy people! Like the ostrich, they bury their heads in the sand, and imagine that everything around has disappeared. A number of liberal publicists who month after month proclaimed to the world their triumph over the collapse and even disappearance of Marxism; a number of liberal newspapers (*St. Peterburgskiye Vyedomosti, Russkiye Vyedomosti* and many others) which encourage the liberals who bring to the workers the Brentano conception of the class struggle and the trade-union conception of politics—the galaxy of critics of Marxism, whose real tendencies were so very well disclosed by the *Credo* and whose literary products alone circulate freely in Russia—the animation among revolutionary *non*-Social-Democratic tendencies, particularly after the February and March events—all these, of course, are mere phantoms! Of course, it has nothing at all to do with bourgeois democracy!

Rabocheye Dyelo and the authors of the Economic Letter published in *Iskra* No. 12, should "ponder over the question as to why the events in the spring excited such animation among the revolutionary non-Social-Democratic tendencies instead of increasing the authority and the prestige of Social-Democracy. The reason was that we failed to cope with our tasks. The masses of the workers proved to be more active than we, we lacked adequately trained revolutionary leaders and organisers aware of the mood prevailing among all the oppositional strata and able to march at the head of the movement, convert the spontaneous demonstration into a political demonstration, broaden its political character, etc. Under such circumstances, our backwardness will inevitably be taken advantage of by the more mobile and more energetic non-Social-

---

* Suggesting that they are subservient.—*Ed.*

** This is a reference to the "concrete Russian conditions which fatalistically impel the labour movement on the revolutionary path." But these people refuse to understand that the revolutionary path of the labour movement might not be a Social-Democratic path! When absolutism reigned in Western Europe, the entire Western European bourgeoisie "impelled" and deliberately impelled the workers on the path of revolution. We, Social-Democrats, however, cannot be satisfied with that. And if we, by any means whatever, degrade Social-Democratic politics to the level of spontaneous trade-union politics, we, by that, play into the hands of bourgeois democracy.

Democratic revolutionists, and the workers, no matter how strenuously and self-sacrificingly they may fight the police and the troops, no matter how revolutionary they may act, will prove to be merely the rearguard of bourgeois democracy, and not the vanguard of Social-Democracy. Take, for example, the German Social-Democrats, whose weak sides alone our Economists desire to emulate. Why is it that *not a single* political event takes place in Germany without adding to the authority and prestige of Social-Democracy? Because Social-Democracy is always found to be in advance of all others in their revolutionary estimation of any event and in their championship of every protest against tyranny. It does not soothe itself by arguments about the economic struggle bringing the workers up against their own lack of rights, and about concrete conditions fatalistically impelling the labour movement on the path of revolution. It intervenes in every sphere and in every question of social and political life. In the matter of Wilhelm's refusal to endorse a bourgeois progressive as city mayor (our Economists have not yet managed to convince the Germans that this in fact is a compromise with liberalism!); in the question of the law against the publication of "immoral" publications and pictures; in the question of the government's influencing the election of the professors, etc., etc., everywhere Social-Democracy is found to be ahead of all others, rousing political discontent among all classes, rousing the sluggards, pushing on the laggards and providing a wealth of material for the development of the political consciousness and political activity of the proletariat. The result of all this is that even the avowed enemies of Socialism are filled with respect for this advanced political fighter and sometimes an important document from bourgeois and even from bureaucratic and Court circles makes its way by some miraculous means into the editorial office of *Vorwaerts*.

This, then, is the explanation of the seeming "contradiction" that passes the understanding of *Rabocheye Dyelo* to such an extent that it raises its arms and cries: "Masquerade"! Is it not a shocking thing: We, *Rabocheye Dyelo*, place the mass labour movement as the **cornerstone** (and printed in heavy type!); we warn all and sundry against belittling the significance of the spontaneous movement; we desire to give the economic struggle itself, *itself, itself*, a political character; we desire to maintain close and organic contact with the proletarian struggle! And yet we are told that we **are** preparing the ground for converting the labour movement into an instrument of bourgeois democracy! And who says this? People who "compromise" with liberalism, intervene in every "liberal" question (what a gross misunderstanding of the "organic contacts with the proletarian struggle"!), who devote so much attention to the students and even (Oh horror!) to the Zemstvoists! People who wish to devote a greater (compared with the Economists) percentage of their efforts to activity among non-proletarian classes of the population! Is not this a "masquerade"?

Poor *Rabocheye Dyelo!* Will it ever find the solution of this complicated puzzle?

IV

THE PRIMITIVENESS OF THE ECONOMISTS AND THE
ORGANISATION OF REVOLUTIONISTS

Rabocheye Dyelo's assertions—which we have analysed—that
the economic struggle is the most widely applicable means of political agitation and that our task now is to give the economic struggle
itself a political character, etc., not only express a restricted view
of our political tasks, but also of our *organisational tasks.* The
"economic struggle against the employers and the government"
does not in the least require—and therefore such a struggle can
never give rise to—an All-Russian centralised organisation that will
combine, in a general attack, all the numerous manifestations of
political opposition, protest and indignation, an organisation that
will consist of professional revolutionaries and be led by the real
political leaders of the whole people. And this can be easily understood. The character of the organisation of every institution is
naturally and inevitably determined by the character of the activity
that institution conducts. Consequently, *Rabocheye Dyelo,* by the
above-analysed assertions, not only sanctifies and legitimatises the
narrowness of political activity, but also the narrowness of organisational work. And in this case also, as always, its consciousness
shrinks before spontaneity. And yet, subservience to spontaneously rising forms of organisation, the lack of appreciation of the
narrowness and primitiveness of our organisational work, of our
"primitive methods" in this most important sphere, the lack of such
appreciation, I say, is a very serious complaint that our movement
suffers from. It is not a complaint that comes with decline, of
course, it is a complaint that comes with growth. But it is precisely
at the present time, when the wave of spontaneous indignation is, as
it were, lashing us leaders and organisers of the movement, that a
most irreconcilable struggle must be carried on against all defence
of sluggishness, against any legitimisation of restriction in this
matter, and it is particularly necessary to rouse in all those par-
ticipating in the practical work, in all who are just thinking of
taking it up, discontent with the *primitive methods* that prevail
among us and unshakable determination to get rid of them.

A. What Are Primitive Methods?

We shall try to answer this question by describing the activity of a typical Social-Democratic circle of the period of 1894-1901. We have already referred to the manner in which the students became absorbed in Marxism at that period. Of course, these students were not so much interested in Marxism as a theory; they were interested in it because it provided the answer to the question: "What is to be done?"; because it was a call to march against the enemy. And these young warriors marched to battle with astonishingly primitive equipment and training. In a vast number of cases, they had almost no equipment, and absolutely no training. They marched to war like peasants from the plough, snatching up a club. A students' circle with no contacts with the old members of the movement, no contacts with circles in other districts, or even in other parts of the same city (or with other schools), without the various sections of the revolutionary work being in any way organised, having no systematic plan of activity covering any length of time, establishes contacts with the workers and sets to work. The circle gradually expands its propaganda and agitation; by its activities it wins the sympathies of a rather large circle of workers and of a certain section of the educated classes, which provides it with money and from which the "committee" recruits new groups of members. The fascination which the committee (or the League of Struggle) exercises on the youth increases, its sphere of activity becomes wider and its activities expand quite spontaneously: the very people who a year or a few months previously had spoken at the gatherings of the students' circle and discussed the question, "Whither?" who established and maintained contacts with the workers, wrote and published leaflets, established contacts with other groups of revolutionists and procured literature, now set to work to establish a local newspaper, begin to talk about organising demonstrations, and finally, commence open conflicts (these open conflicts may, according to circumstances, take the form of issuing the very first agitational leaflet, or the first newspaper, or of organising the first demonstration). And usually, the first action ends in immediate and complete defeat. Immediate and complete, precisely because these open conflicts were not the result of a systematic and carefully thought-out and gradually prepared plan for a prolonged and stubborn struggle, but simply the spontaneous growth of traditional circle work; because naturally, the police, almost in every case, knew the principal leaders of the local movement, for they had already "recommended" themselves to the police in their school-days, and the latter only waited for a convenient day to make their raid. They gave the circle sufficient time to develop their work so that they may obtain a palpable *corpus delicti,** and always allowed several of the persons known to them to remain at liberty for *razvodka* (which, I believe is the technical term used both by our people and by the gendarmes) ** One cannot help comparing this kind of warfare with that conducted by a mob of peasants armed with clubs against modern troops. One can only express astonishment at the virility displayed by the movement which expanded, grew and won victories in spite of the lack of training among the fighters. It is true that from the historical point-of-view, the primitiveness of equipment was not only inevitable at first, but even *legitimate* as one of the conditions for the wide recruiting of fighters, but as soon as serious operations commenced (and they commenced in fact with the strikes in the summer of 1896), the defects in our fighting organisations made themselves felt to an increasing extent. Thrown into consternation at first and committing a number of mistakes (for example, its appeal to the public describing the misdeeds of the Socialists, or the deportation of the workers from the capital to the provincial industrial centres) the government very soon adapted itself to the new conditions of the struggle and managed to place its perfectly equipped detachments of agent-provocateurs, spies, and gendarmes in the required places. Raids became so frequent, affected such a vast number of people, and cleared out the local circles so thoroughly, that the masses of the workers literally lost all their leaders, the movement assumed an incredibly sporadic character, and it became utterly impossible to established continuity and connectedness in the work. The fact that the local active workers were hopelessly scattered, the casual manner in which the membership of the circles were recruited, the lack of training in and narrow outlook on theoretical, political and organisational questions were all the inevitable result of the conditions described above. Things reached such a pass

* Offence within the meaning of the law.—*Ed.*
** Literally for "breeding purposes," *i. e.,* to breed more victims for the police net. By allowing them to be at liberty and by shadowing their movements, the police were able to use them as innocent tools to betray the whereabouts of other revolutionists as yet unknown to them.—*Ed.*

that in several places the workers, because of our lack of stamina and ability to maintain secrecy, began to lose faith in the intelligentsia and to avoid them: The intellectuals, they said, are much too careless and lay themselves open to police raids!

Any one who has the slightest knowledge of the movement knows that these primitive methods at last began to be recognised as a disease by all thinking Social-Democrats. And in order that the reader, who is not acquainted with the movement, may have no grounds for thinking that we are "inventing" a special stage or special disease of the movement, we shall refer once again to the witness we have already quoted. No doubt we shall be excused for the length of the passage quoted:

While the gradual transition to wider practical activity [writes B-v in *Rabocheye Dyelo*, No. 6], a transition which is closely connected with the general transitional period through which the Russian labour movement is now passing, is a characteristic feature . . . there is, however, another and not less interesting feature in the general mechanism of the Russian workers' revolution. We refer to the *general lack of revolutionary forces fit for action* * which is felt not only in St. Petersburg, but throughout the whole of Russia. With the general revival of the labour movement, with the general development of the working masses, with the growing frequency of strikes, and with the mass labour struggle becoming more and more open, the intensification of government persecution, arrests, deportation and exile, *this lack of highly skilled revolutionary forces is becoming more and more marked* and, without a doubt, *must leave deep traces upon the general character of the movement.* Many strikes take place without the revolutionary organisations exercising any strong and direct influence upon them. . . . A shortage of agitational leaflets and illegal literature is felt. . . . The workers' circles are left without agitators. . . . Simultaneously, there is a constant shortage of funds. In a word, *the growth of the labour movement is outstripping the growth and development of the revolutionary organisations.* The numerical strength of the active revolutionists is too small to enable them to concentrate in themselves all the influence exercised upon the whole of the discontented masses of labour, or to give this unrest even a shadow of symmetry and organisation. . . . Separate circles, separate revolutionists, scattered, uncombined do not represent a united, strong and disciplined organisation with the planned development of its parts. . . .

Admitting that the immediate organisation of fresh circles to take the place of those that have been broken up, "merely proves the virility of the movement . . . but does not prove the existence of an adequate number of sufficiently fit revolutionary workers," the author concludes:

The lack of practical training among the St. Petersburg revolutionists is seen in the results of their work. The recent trials, especially that of the Self-

* All italics ours.

Emancipation group and the Labour versus Capital group clearly showed that the young agitator, unacquainted with the details of the conditions of labour and, consequently, unacquainted with the conditions under which agitation must be carried on in a given factory, ignorant of the principles of conspiracy, and understanding only the general principles of Social-Democracy [and it is a question whether he understands them] is able to carry on his work for perhaps four, five, or six months. Then come arrests, which frequently lead to the break-up of the whole organisation, or at all events, of part of it. The question arises, therefore, can the group conduct successful and fruitful activity if its existence is measured by months? Obviously, the defects of the existing organisations cannot be wholly ascribed to the transitional period. . . . Obviously, the numerical and above all the qualitative strength of the organisations operating is not of little importance, and the first task our Social-Democrats must undertake is *effectively to combine the organisations and make a strict selection of their membership.*

B. Primitive Methods and Economism

We must now deal with the question that undoubtedly must have arisen in the mind of every reader. Have these primitive methods, which are a complaint of growth that affect *the whole of the movement,* any connection with Economism, which is *only one* of the tendencies in Russian Social-Democracy? We think that they have. The lack of practical training, the lack of ability to carry on organisational work is certainly common *to us all,* including those who have stood unswervingly by the point-of-view of revolutionary Marxism right from the very outset. And, of course, no one can blame the practical workers for their lack of practical training. But, the term "primitive methods" embraces something more than mere lack of training: It embraces the restrictedness of revolutionary work generally, the failure to understand that a good organisation of revolutionists cannot be built up on the basis of such restricted work, and lastly—and most important—it embraces the attempts to justify this restrictedness and to elevate it to a special "theory," *i. e.,* subservience to spontaneity in this matter also. As soon as such attempts were observed, it became certain that primitive methods are connected with Economism and that we shall never eliminate this restrictedness of our organisational activity until we eliminate Economism generally (*i. e.,* the narrow conception of Marxian theory, of the rôle of Social-Democracy, and of its political tasks). And these attempts were revealed in a two-fold direction. Some began to say: The labour masses have not yet themselves brought up the broad and militant tasks that the revolutionists desire to "impose" upon them; they must continue for the time being to fight for *immediate* political demands, to conduct "the economic struggle against the employers and the government" * (this mass struggle "easily understood" by these masses naturally corresponds to an organisation "easily accessible" to the most untrained youth). Others, far removed from "gradualness," began to say: We can and must "bring about a political revolution," but there is no reason whatever for building a strong organisation of revolutionists that would train revolutionists for the stalwart and stubborn struggle, in order to bring this revolution about. All we need do is to snatch up the "easily understood" wooden club, the acquaintance with which we have already made. Speaking, without metaphor, it means—we must organise a general strike,** or we must stimulate the "spiritless" progress of the labour movement by means of "excitative terror." *** Both these tendencies, the opportunist and the "revolutionary," bow to the prevailing primitiveness; neither believe that it can be eliminated, neither understand our primary and most imperative practical task, namely, to establish *an organisation of revolutionists* capable of maintaining the energy, the stability and continuity of the political struggle.

We have just quoted the words of B-v: "The growth of the labour movement is outstripping the growth and development of the revolutionary organisations." This "valuable remark of a close observer" (*Rabocheye Dyelo's* comment on B-v's article) has a twofold value for us. It proves that we were right in our opinion that the principal cause of the present crisis in Russian Social-Democracy is that the *leaders* ("ideologists," revolutionists, Social-Democrats) *lag behind the spontaneous rising of the masses.* It shows that all the arguments advanced by the authors of the Economic Letter in *Iskra*, No. 12, by B. Krichevsky, and by Martynov, about the dangers of belittling the significance of the spontaneous elements, about the drab every-day struggles, about the tactics-process, etc., are nothing more than a glorification and defence of primitive methods. These people, who cannot pronounce the word "theoretician" without a contemptuous grimace, who describe their genuflections to common lack of training and ignorance as "sensitiveness

---

* *Rabochaya Mysl* and *Rabocheye Dyelo*, especially the *Reply* to Plekhanov.
** See *Who Will Bring About the Political Revolution?* A symposium published in Russia entitled, *The Proletarian Struggle.* Re-issued by the Kiev Committee.
*** *Regeneration of Revolutionism* and *Svoboda.*

to life," reveal in practice a failure to understand our most imperative *practical* task. To laggards they shout: Keep in step! don't run ahead! To people suffering from a lack of energy and initiative in organisational work, from lack of "plans" for wide and bold organisational work, they shout about the "tactics-process"! The most serious sin we commit is that we *degrade* our political and *our organisational* tasks to the level of immediate, "palpable," "concrete" interests of the every-day economic struggle; and yet they keep singing to us the old song: Give the economic struggle itself a political character. We say again: This kind of thing displays as much "sensitiveness to life" as was displayed by the hero in the popular fable who shouted to a passing funeral procession: May you never get to your destination.*

Recall the matchless, truly "Narcissus"-like superciliousness with which these wiseacres lectured Plekhanov about the "workers' *circles* generally" [*sic!*] being "incapable of fulfilling political tasks in the real and *practical* sense of the word, *i. e.,* the sense of expedient and successful *practical* struggle for political demands." [*Rabocheye Dyelo's Reply*, p. 24.] There are circles and circles, gentlemen! Circles of "kustars," ** of course, are incapable of fulfilling political tasks and never will be, until they realise the primitiveness of their methods and abandon it. If besides this, these amateurs are enamoured of their primitive methods, and insist on writing the word "practical" in italics, and imagine that practicality demands that their tasks be degraded to the level of understanding of the most backward strata of the masses, then they are hopeless, of course, and certainly cannot *fulfil general political tasks*. But circles of heroes, like those formed by Alexeyev and Myshkin, Khalturin and Zhelyabov, are able to fulfil political tasks in the genuine and most practical sense of the term, because their passionate preaching meets with response among the spontaneously awakened masses, because their seething energy rouses a corresponding and sustained energy among the revolutionary class. Plekhanov was a thousand times right not only when he pointed to this revolutionary class, not only when he proved that its spontaneous awakening was inevitable, but also when he set the "workers' circles" a great and lofty political task. But you refer to the mass movement that has sprung up since that time in order to

---

* This refers to a popular fable about "Ivan the Fool."—*Ed.*

** Kustars—handicraftsmen employing primitive methods in their work.—*Ed.*

degrade this task, in order to *curtail* the energy and scope of activity of the "workers' circles." If you are not amateurs enamoured of your primitive methods, what are you then? You clutch at your practicality, but you fail to see what every Russian practical worker knows, namely, the miracles that the energy, not only of circles, but even of individual persons is able to perform in the revolutionary cause. Or do you think that our movements cannot produce heroes like those that were produced by the movement in the seventies? If so, why do you think so? Because we lack training? But we are training ourselves, will train ourselves and we will be trained! Unfortunately it is true that scum has formed on the surface of the stagnant water of the "economic struggle against the employers and the government"; there are people among us who kneel in prayer to spontaneity, gazing with awe upon the "posteriors" of the Russian proletariat (as Plekhanov expresses it). But we will remove this scum. The time has come when Russian revolutionists, led by a genuine revolutionary theory, relying upon the genuinely revolutionary and spontaneously awakening class, can at last—at last!—rise to their full height and exert their giant strength to the utmost. All that is required in order that this may be so is that the masses of our practical workers and the still larger masses of those who dream of doing practical work even while still at school shall meet with scorn and ridicule any suggestion that may be made to degrade our political tasks, and to restrict the scope of our organisational work. And we will achieve that, don't you worry, gentlemen!

In the article, "Where to Begin," that I wrote in opposition to *Rabocheye Dyelo*, I said: "Tactics in relation to some special question, or in relation to some detail of party organisation may be changed in twenty-four hours; but views as to whether a militant organisation, and political agitation among the masses, is necessary at all times or not cannot be changed in twenty-four hours, or even in twenty-four months for that matter." * To this *Rabocheye Dyelo* replied: "This is the only charge *Iskra* has levelled against us that claims to be based on facts, and even that is totally without foundation. Readers of *Rabocheye Dyelo* know very well that right from the outset we not only called for political agitation, without

* See "Where to Begin," *The Iskra Period*, Book I, p. 110.—*Ed.*

waiting for the appearance of *Iskra* * . . ." [and while doing so, you said that it was "impossible to impose on the mass labour movement, or on the workers' circles, the primary political task of overthrowing absolutism," that the only task they could carry out was to struggle for immediate political demands, and that "immediate political demands are understood by the masses after a strike, or at all events, after a few strikes"] ". . . but in the publications that we procured from abroad for the comrades working in Russia, provided the *only* Social-Democratic political and agitational material . . ." [and this only Social-Democratic material, the only political agitation that was carried on by you at all widely, was based exclusively on the economic struggle, and you even went so far as to claim that this restricted agitation was "the most widely applicable." And you fail to observe, gentlemen, that your own arguments—that this was the only material provided—proves the necessity for *Iskra's* appearance, and proves how necessary it is for *Iskra* to oppose *Rabocheye Dyelo*]. ". . . On the other hand, our publishing activity really prepared the ground for the tactical unity of the party. . . ." [Unity in the conviction that tactics are a process of growth of party tasks that grow together with the party? A precious unity indeed!] ". . . and by that rendered possible the creation of a 'militant organisation' for which the League did all that an organisation abroad could do." [*Rabocheye Dyelo*, No. 10, p. 15.] A vain attempt at evasion! I would never dream of denying that you did all you possibly could. I have asserted and assert now, that the *limits* of what is "possible" for you to do are restricted by the narrowness of your outlook. It is ridiculous to talk about a "militant organisation" fighting for "immediate political demands," or conducting "the economic struggle against the employers and the government."

But if the reader wishes to see the pearls of Economist primitive methods, he must, of course, turn from the eclectic and vacillating *Rabocheye Dyelo* to the consistent and determined *Rabochaya Mysl.* In its Special Supplement, p. 13, R. M. wrote:

Now two words about the so-called revolutionary intelligentsia proper. It is true that on more than one occasion it proved that it was quite prepared to "enter into determined battle with tsarism!" The unfortunate thing, however, is, that, ruthlessly persecuted by the political police, our revolutionary intelligentsia imagined that the battle with this political police was a political struggle with the autocracy. That is why, to this day, it cannot understand "where the forces for the fight against the autocracy are to be obtained."

What matchless and magnificent contempt for the struggle with the police the worshippers (in the worst sense of the word) of the *spontaneous* movement display, do they not? They are prepared to *justify* our inability to organise secretly by the argument that with the spontaneous growth of the mass movement, it is not at all important for us to fight against the political police!! Not many are prepared to subscribe to this monstrous conclusion; our defects in revolutionary organisation has become too urgent a matter to permit them to do that. Martynov, for example, would also refuse to subscribe to this, but in his case it is only because he is unable, or lacks the courage, to think out his ideas to their logical conclusion. Indeed, does the "task" of prompting the masses to put forward concrete demands promising palpable results call for special efforts to create a stable, centralised, militant, organisation of revolutionists? Cannot such a "task" be carried out even by masses who do not "fight at all against the political police"? Moreover, can this task be fulfilled unless, in addition to the few leaders, it is undertaken by the workers (the overwhelming majority), who in fact are *incapable* of "fighting against the political police"? Such workers, average people of the masses, are capable of displaying enormous energy and self-sacrifice in strikes and in street battles, with the police and troops, and are capable (in fact, are alone capable) of *determining* the whole outcome of our movement—but the struggle against the *political* police requires special qualities; it can be conducted only by *professional* revolutionists. And we must not only see to it that the masses "advance" concrete demands, but also that the masses of the workers "advance" an increasing number of such professional revolutionists from their own ranks. Thus we have reached the question of the relation between an organisation of professional revolutionists and the pure and simple labour movement. Although this question has found little reflection in literature, it has greatly engaged us "politicians," in conversations and controversies with those comrades who gravitate more or less towards Economism. It is a question that deserves special treatment. But before taking it up we shall deal with one other quotation in order to illustrate the position we hold in regard to the connection between primitiveness and Economism.

In his *Reply*, N. N. wrote: "The Emancipation of Labour group demands direct struggle against the government without first considering where the material forces for this struggle are to be obtained, and without indicating *'the path of the struggle.'*" Emphasising the last words, the author adds the following footnote to the word "path": "This cannot be explained by the conspiratorial aims pursued, because the programme does not refer to secret plotting but to a *mass movement*. The masses cannot proceed by secret paths. Can we conceive of a secret strike? Can we conceive of secret demonstrations and petitions?" [*Vademecum*, p. 59.] Thus, the author approaches quite close to the question of the "material forces" (organisers of strikes and demonstrations) and to the "paths" of the struggle, but nevertheless, is still in a state of consternation, because he "worships" the mass movement, *i. e.*, he regards it as something that *relieves* us of the necessity for carrying on revolutionary activity and not as something that should embolden us and *stimulate* our revolutionary activity. Secret strikes are impossible —for those who take a direct and immediate part in them, but a strike may remain (and in the majority of cases does remain) a "secret" to the masses of the Russian workers, because the government takes care to cut all communication between strikers, takes care to prevent all news of strikes from spreading. Now here indeed is a special "struggle against the political police" required, a struggle that can never be conducted by such large masses as usually take part in strikes. Such a struggle must be organised, according to "all the rules of the art," by people who are professionally engaged in revolutionary activity. The fact that the masses are spontaneously entering the movement does not make the organisation of this struggle *less necessary*. On the contrary, it makes it *more necessary;* for we Socialists would be failing in our duty to the masses if we did not prevent the police from making a secret of (and if we did not ourselves sometimes secretly prepare) every strike and every demonstration. *And we will succeed in doing this,* precisely because the spontaneously awakening masses will *also advance from their own ranks* increasing numbers of "professional revolutionists" (that is, if we are not so foolish as to advise the workers to keep on marking time).

C. Organisation of Workers, and Organisation of Revolutionists

It is only natural that a Social-Democrat who conceives the political struggle as being identical with the "economic struggle against the employers and the government," should conceive "organisation of revolutionists" as being more or less identical with "organisation of workers." And this, in fact, is what actually happens; so that when we talk about organisation, we literally talk in different tongues. I recall a conversation I once had with a fairly consistent Economist, with whom I had not been previously acquainted. We were discussing the brochure *Who Will Make the Political Revolution?* and we were very soon agreed that the principal defect in that brochure was that it ignored the question of organisation. We were beginning to think that we were in complete agreement with each other—but as the conversation proceeded, it became clear that we were talking of different things. My interlocutor accused the author of the brochure just mentioned of ignoring strike funds, mutual-aid societies, etc.; whereas I had in mind an organisation of revolutionists, as an essential factor in "making" the political revolution. After that became clear, I hardly remember a single question of importance upon which I was in agreement with that Economist!

What was the source of our disagreement? It is the fact that on questions of organisation and politics the Economists are forever lapsing from Social-Democracy into trade unionism. The political struggle carried on by the Social-Democrats is far more extensive and complex than the economic struggle the workers carry on against the employers and the government. Similarly (and indeed for that reason), the organisation of revolutionary Social-Democrats must inevitably *differ* from the organisations of the workers designed for the latter struggle. The workers' organisations must in the first place be trade organisations; secondly, they must be as wide as possible; and thirdly, they must be as public as conditions will allow (here, of course, I have only autocratic Russia in mind). On the other hand, the organisations of revolutionists must be comprised first and foremost of people whose profession is that of revolutionists (that is why I speak of organisations of *revolutionists*, meaning revolutionary Social-Democrats). As this is the common feature of the members of such an organisation, *all dis-*

tinctions as between workers and intellectuals, and certainly distinctions of trade and profession, must be dropped. Such an organisation must of necessity be not too extensive and as secret as possible. Let us examine this three-fold distinction.

In countries where political liberty exists the distinction between a labour union and a political organisation is clear, as is the distinction between trade unions and Social-Democracy. The relation of the latter to the former will naturally vary in each country according to historical, legal and other conditions—it may be more or less close or more or less complex (in our opinion it should be as close and simple as possible); but trade-union organisations are certainly not in the least identical with the Social-Democratic party organisations in those countries. In Russia, however, the yoke of autocracy appears at first glance to obliterate all distinctions between a Social-Democratic organisation and trade unions, because *all* trade unions and *all* circles are prohibited, and because the principal manifestation and weapon of the workers' economic struggle—the strike—is regarded as a crime (and sometimes even as a political crime!). Conditions in our country, therefore, strongly "impel" the workers who are conducting the economic struggle to concern themselves with political questions. They also "impel" the Social-Democrats to confuse trade unionism with Social-Democracy (and our Krichevskys, Martynovs and their like, while speaking enthusiastically of the first kind of "impelling," fail to observe the "impelling" of the second kind). Indeed, picture to yourselves the people who are immersed ninety-nine per cent in "the economic struggle against the employers and the government." Some of them never, *during the whole course of their activity* (four to six months), thought of the necessity for a more complex organisation of revolutionists; others, perhaps, come across the fairly widely distributed revisionist literature, from which they convince themselves of the profound importance of "the drab daily struggle." Still others will be carried away, perhaps, by the seductive idea of showing the world a new example of "close and organic contact with the proletarian struggle"—contact between the trade-union and Social-Democratic movements. Such people would perhaps argue that the later a country enters into the arena of capitalism, the more the Socialists in that country may take part in and support the trade-union movement, and the less reason is there for non-Social-Democratic trade unions. So far, the argument is absolutely correct:

unfortunately, however, some go beyond that and hint at the complete fusion of Social-Democracy with trade unionism. We shall soon see, from the example of the statutes of the St. Petersburg League of Struggle, what a harmful effect this has upon our plans of organisation.

The workers' organisations for carrying on the economic struggle should be trade-union organisations; every Social-Democratic worker should, as far as possible, support and actively work inside these organisations. That is true. But it would be far from being to our interest to demand that only Social-Democrats be eligible for membership in the trade unions. The only effect of this, if it were attempted, would be to restrict our influence over the masses. Let every worker who understands the necessity for organisation, in order to carry on the struggle against the employers and the government, join the trade unions. The very objects of the trade unions would be unattainable unless they united all who have attained at least this elementary level of understanding, and unless they were extremely wide organisations. The wider these organisations are, the wider our influence over them will be. They will then be influenced not only by the "spontaneous" development of the economic struggle, but also by the direct and conscious action of the Socialists on their comrades in the unions. But a wide organisation cannot be a strictly secret organisation (since the latter demands far greater training than is required for the economic struggle). How is the contradiction between the necessity for a large membership and the necessity for strictly secret methods to be reconciled? How are we to make the trade unions as public as possible? Generally speaking, there are perhaps only two ways to this end: Either the trade unions become legalised (which in some countries precedes the legalisation of the Socialist and political unions), or the organisation is kept a secret one, but so "free" and "loose" that the need for secret methods become almost negligible as far as the mass of the members are concerned.

The legalisation of the non-Socialist and non-political labour unions in Russia has already begun, and there is no doubt that every advance our rapidly growing Social-Democratic working-class movement makes will increase and encourage the attempts at legalisation. These attempts proceed for the most part from supporters of the existing order, but they will proceed also from the workers themselves and from the liberal intellectuals. The banner of legality has already been unfurled by the Vassilyevs and the Zubatovs. Support has been promised by the Ozerovs and the Wormses; and followers of the new tendency are to be found even among the workers. Henceforth, we must reckon with this tendency. How are we to reckon with it? About this there can be no two opinions among Social-Democrats. We must constantly expose any part played in this movement by the Zubatovs and the Vassilyevs, the gendarmes and the priests, and explain to the workers what their intentions are. We must also expose the conciliatory, "harmonious" undertones that will be heard in the speeches delivered by liberal politicians at the legal meetings of the workers, irrespective of whether they proceed from an earnest conviction as to the desirability of the peaceful co-operation of the classes, whether they proceed from a desire to curry favour with the employers, or are simply the result of not being able to do otherwise. We must also warn the workers against the traps often set by the police, who at such open meetings and permitted societies spy out the "hotheads," and who, through the medium of the legal organisations, endeavour to plant their agent-provocateurs in the illegal organisations.

But while doing all this, we must not forget that *in the long run*, the legalisation of the working class movement will be to our advantage, and not to the Zubatovs. On the contrary, our campaign of exposure will help to separate the tares from the wheat. What the tares are, we have already indicated. By the wheat we mean, attracting the attention of increasing numbers of the more backward sections of the workers to social and political questions, and to freeing ourselves, the revolutionists, from functions which are essentially legal (the distribution of legal books, mutual aid, etc.), the development of which will inevitably provide us with an increasing quantity of material for agitation. Looked at from this point of view, we may say, and we should say to the Zubatovs and the Ozerovs, "Keep at it, gentlemen, do your best!" We shall expose your efforts to place a trap in the path of the workers (either by way of direct provocation, or by the "honest" corruption of the workers with the aid of Struveism), but we shall be grateful for every real step forward even if it is timid and vacillating; we shall say: Please continue! A real step forward can only result in a real, if small, extension of the workers' field of action. And every such extension must be to our advantage and help to hasten the advent of legal societies, not of the kind in which agents-provocateurs hunt for Socialists, but of the kind in which Socialists will hunt for adherents. In a word, our task is to fight down the tares. It is not our business to grow wheat in flower-pots. By pulling up the tares, we clear the soil for the wheat. And while the old-fashioned folk are tending their flower-pot crops, we must prepare reapers, not only to cut down the tares of to-day, but also to reap the wheat of to-morrow.*

Legalisation, therefore, will *not solve* the problem of creating a trade-union organisation that will be as public and as extensive as possible (but we would be extremely glad if the Zubatovs and the Ozerovs provided even a partial opportunity for such a solution—to which end we must fight them as strenuously as possible!). There only remains the path of secret trade-union organisation; and *we must* offer every possible assistance to the workers, who (as we definitely know) have already adopted this path. Trade-union organisations may not only be of tremendous value in developing and consolidating the economic struggle, but may also become a very useful auxiliary to the political, agitational and revolutionary organisations.

In order to achieve this purpose, and in order to guide the nascent trade-union movement in the direction the Social-Democrats desire, we must first fully understand the foolishness of the plan of organisation with which the St. Petersburg Economists have been occupying themselves for nearly five years. That plan is described in the Rules of a Workers' Fund, of July, 1897 [*Listok Rabotnika*, Nos. 9 and 10, p. 46, in *Rabochaya Mysl*, No. 1], and also in the Rules for a Trade Union Workers' Organisation, of October, 1900 [special leaflet printed in St. Petersburg and quoted in *Iskra*, No. 1]. The fundamental error contained in both these sets of rules is that they give a detailed formulation of a wide workers' organisation and confuse the latter with the organisation of revolutionists. Let

---

* *Iskra's* campaign against the tares evoked the following angry outbreak on the part of *Rabocheye Dyelo*: "For *Iskra*, the signs of the times lie not in the great events of the spring, but in the miserable attempts of the agents of Zubatov to 'legalise' the working-class movement. It fails to see that these facts tell against it and prove that the working-class movement is assuming menacing proportions in the eyes of the government." [*Two Congresses*, p. 27.] For this we have to blame the "dogmatism" of the orthodox Marxists who ignore the imperative demands of life. They obstinately refuse to see the yard-high wheat and are fighting down the inch-high tares! Does this not reveal a "distorted sense of perspective in regard to the Russian working-class movement"? [*ibid*, p. 27.]

us take the last-mentioned set of rules, since it is drawn up in greater detail. The body of it consists of *fifty-two* paragraphs. Twenty-three paragraphs deal with structure, the method of conducting business, and the competence of the "workers circles," which are to be organised in every factory ("not more than ten persons") and which elect "central (factory) groups." "The central group," says paragraph 2, "observes all that goes on in its factory or workshop and keeps a record of events. . . ." "The central group presents to the contributors a monthly report on the state of the funds" (Par. 17), etc. Ten paragraphs are devoted to the "district organisation" and nineteen to the highly complex connection between the Committee of the Workers' Organisation and the Committee of the St. Petersburg League of Struggle (elected by each district and by the "executive groups"—"groups of propagandists for maintaining contact with the provinces and with exiles abroad, and for managing stores, publications and funds").

Social-Democracy = "executive groups" connected with the economic struggle of the workers! It would be difficult to find a more striking illustration than this of how far the Economists' ideas deviate from Social-Democracy on the question of trade unionism, and how foreign to them is the idea that a Social-Democrat must concern himself first and foremost with an organisation of revolutionists, capable of guiding the *whole* proletarian struggle for emancipation. To talk of "the political emancipation of the working class" and the struggle against "tsarist despotism," and at the same time to write statutes like these, indicates a complete failure to understand what the real political tasks of the Social-Democrats are. Not one of the fifty or so paragraphs reveals the slightest glimmer of understanding that it is necessary to conduct the widest possible political agitation among the masses, an agitation that deals with every phase of Russian absolutism, and with every aspect of the various social classes in Russia. Rules like these are of no use even for the achievement of trade union aims, quite apart from political aims, for that requires organisation *according to trade,* and yet the rules do not contain a single reference to this.

But most characteristic of all, perhaps, is the amazing top-heaviness of the whole "system," which attempts to unite every factory with the "committee" by a long string of uniform and ludicrously petty rules and a three-stage system of election. Hemmed in by the narrow outlook of Economism, the mind is lost in details which positively reek of red tape and bureaucracy. In practice, of course, three-fourths of the clauses are impossible of application; moreover, a "conspiratorial" organisation of this kind, with its central group in each factory, will render the work of the gendarmes extraordinarily easy. Our Polish comrades have already passed through a similar phase in their own movement, when everybody was extremely enthusiastic about the extensive organisation of workers' funds; but these ideas were very quickly abandoned when it was found that the funds only provided rich harvests for the gendarmes. If we are out for wide workers' organisations, and not for wide arrests, if it is not our purpose to provide satisfaction to the gendarmes, these organisations must remain absolutely loose and not bound by any strict rules. . . . But will they be able to function? Well, let us see what the functions are: ". . . To observe all that goes on in the factory and keep a record of events" (Par. 2 of the Rules). Must that really be formulated in a set of rules? Could not the purpose be better served by correspondence conducted in the illegal papers and without setting up special groups? ". . . To lead the struggles of the workers for the improvement of their workshop conditions" (Par. 3 of the Rules). This, too, need not be strictly formulated. Any agitator with any intelligence at all can gather what the demands of the workers are in the course of ordinary conversation and transmit them to a narrow—not a wide—organisation of revolutionists to be embodied in a leaflet; ". . . To organise a fund . . . to which contributions of two kopecks per ruble * should be made (Par. 9) . . . to present monthly reports to the contributors on the state of the funds (Par. 17) . . . to expel members who fail to pay their contributions (Par. 10), and so forth. Why, this is a very paradise for the police; for nothing would be easier than for them to penetrate into the ponderous secrecy of a "central factory fund," confiscate the money and arrest the best members. Would it not be simpler to issue one-kopeck or two-kopeck coupons bearing the official stamp of a well-known (very exclusive and secret) organisation, or to make collections without coupons of any kind and to print reports in a certain agreed code in the legal paper? The object would thereby be attained, but it would be a hundred times more difficult for the gendarmes to pick up clues.

* Of wages earned.—*Ed.*

I could go on analysing the rules, but I think that what has been said will suffice. A small, compact core, consisting of reliable, experienced and hardened workers, with responsible agents in the principal districts and connected by all the rules of strict secrecy with the organisations of revolutionists, can, with the wide support of the masses and without an elaborate set of rules, perform *all* the functions of a trade-union organisation, and perform them, moreover, in the manner Social-Democrats desire. Only in this way can we secure the *consolidation* and development of a *Social-Democratic* trade-union movement, in spite of the gendarmes.

It may be objected that an organisation which is so loose that it is not even formulated, and which even has no enrolled and registered members, cannot be called an organisation at all. That may very well be. I am not out for names. But this "organisation without members" can do everything that is required, and will, from the very outset, guarantee the closest contact between our future trade unionists and Socialism. Only an incorrigible utopian would want a *wide* organisation of workers, with elections, reports, universal suffrage, etc., under autocracy.

The moral to be drawn from this is a simple one. If we begin with the solid foundation of a strong organisation of revolutionists, we can guarantee the stability of the movement as a whole, and carry out the aims of both Social-Democracy and of trade unionism. If, however, we begin with a wide workers' organisation, supposed to be most "accessible" to the masses, when as a matter of fact it will be most accessible to the gendarmes, and will make the revolutionists most accessible to the police, we shall neither achieve the aims of Social-Democracy nor of trade unionism; we shall not escape from our primitiveness, and because we constantly remain scattered and dispersed, we shall make only the trade unions of the Zubatov and Ozerov type most accessible to the masses.

What should be the functions of the organisation of revolutionists? We shall deal with this in detail. But first let us examine a very typical argument advanced by the terrorist, who (sad fate!) in this matter also is in the same boat as the Economist. *Svoboda*— a journal published especially for working men—in its first number, contains an article entitled "Organisation," the author of which tries to defend his friends the Economist workers of Ivanovo-Voznesensk. He writes:

It is a bad thing when the crowd is mute and unenlightened, and when the movement does not proceed from the rank and file. For instance, the students of a university town leave for their homes during the summer and other vacations and immediately the movement comes to a standstill. Can such a workers' movement which has to be pushed on from outside be a real force? Of course not! It has not yet learned to walk, it is still in leading strings. So it is everywhere. The students go off, and everything comes to a standstill. As soon as the cream is skimmed—the milk turns sour. If the "committee" is arrested, everything comes to a standstill until a new one can be formed. And, one never knows what sort of a committee will be set up next —it may be nothing like the former one. The first preached one thing, the second may preach the very opposite. The continuity between yesterday and to-morrow is broken, the experience of the past does not enlighten the future. And all this is because no deep roots have been struck, roots in the crowd; because, instead of having a hundred fools at work, we have ten wise men. Ten wise men can be caught up at a snap; but when the organisation embraces the crowd, everything will proceed from the crowd, and nobody, however zealous, can stop the cause [p. 63].

The facts are described correctly. The above quotation presents a fairly good picture of our primitive methods. But the conclusions drawn from it are worthy of the *Rabochaya Mysl,* both for their stupidity and their political tactlessness. They represent the height of stupidity, because the author confused the philosophical and social-historical question of the "depth" of the "roots" of the movement with the technical and organisational question of the best method of fighting the gendarmes. They represent the height of political tactlessness, because the author, instead of appealing from the bad leaders to the good leaders, appeals from the leaders in general to the "crowd." This is as much an attempt to drag the movement back organisationally, as the idea of substituting political agitation by excitative terrorism is an attempt to drag it back politically.

Indeed, I am experiencing a veritable *embarras de richesses,* and hardly know where to begin to disentangle the confusion *Svoboda* has introduced in this subject. For the sake of clarity, we shall begin by quoting an example. Take the Germans. It will not be denied, I hope, that the German organisations embrace the crowd, that in Germany everything proceeds from the crowd, that the working-class movement there has learned to walk. Yet, observe how this vast crowd of millions values its "dozen" tried political leaders, how firmly it clings to them! Members of the hostile parties in parliament often tease the Socialists by exclaiming: "Fine democrats you are indeed! Your movement is a working-class movement only in name; as a matter of fact it is the same clique of leaders that is always in evidence; Bebel and Liebknecht, year in and year out, and that goes on for decades. Your deputies are supposed to be elected from among the workers, but they are more permanent than the officials appointed by the Emperor!" But the Germans only smile with contempt at these demagogic attempts to set the "crowd" against the "leaders," to arouse turbid and vain instincts in the former, and to rob the movement of its solidity and stability by undermining the confidence of the masses in their "dozen of wise men." The political ideas of the Germans have already developed sufficiently, and they have acquired enough political experience to enable them to understand that without the "dozen" of tried and talented leaders (and talented men are not born by hundreds), professionally trained, schooled by long experience and working in perfect harmony, no class in modern society is capable of conducting a determined struggle. Numerous demagogues in Germany have flattered the "hundred fools," exalted them above the "dozen of wise men," extolled the "mighty fists" of the masses, and (like Most and Hasselmann) have spurred them on to reckless "revolutionary" action and sown distrust towards the tried and trusted leaders. It was only by stubbornly and bitterly combating every symptom of demagogy within the Socialist movement that German Socialism managed to grow and become as strong as it is. Our wiseacres, however, at the very moment when Russian Social-Democracy is passing through a crisis entirely due to our lack of a sufficient number of trained, developed and experienced leaders to guide the spontaneous ferment of the masses, cry out with the profundity of fools, "it is a bad business when the movement does not proceed from the rank and file."

"A committee of students is no good, it is not stable." Quite true. But the conclusion that should be drawn from this is that we must have a committee of professional *revolutionists* and it does not matter whether a student or a worker is capable of qualifying himself as a professional revolutionist. The conclusion you draw, however, is that the working-class movement must not be pushed on from outside! In your political innocence you fail to observe that you are playing into the hands of our Economists and furthering our primitiveness. I would like to ask, what is meant by the students "pushing on" the workers? *All* it means is that the students bring to the worker the fragments of political knowledge they possess, the crumbs of Socialist ideas they have managed to acquire (for the principal intellectual diet of the present-day student, legal Marxism, can furnish only the A. B. C., only the crumbs of knowledge). *Such* "pushing on from outside" can never be too excessive; on the contrary, so far there has been too little, all too little of it in our movement; we have been stewing in our own juice far too long; we have bowed far too slavishly before the spontaneous "economic struggle of the workers against the employers and the government." We professional revolutionists must continue, and will continue, *this kind* of "pushing," and a hundred times more forcibly than we have done hitherto. The very fact that you select so despicable a phrase as "pushing on from outside"—a phrase which cannot but rouse in the workers (at least in the workers who are as ignorant as you are yourselves) a sense of distrust towards *all* who bring them political knowledge and revolutionary experience from outside, and rouse in them an instinctive hostility to such people—proves that you are *demagogues*—and a demagogue is the worst enemy of the working class.

Oh! Don't start howling about my "uncomradely methods" of controversy. I have not the least intention of casting aspersions upon the purity of your intentions. As I have already said, one may be a demagogue out of sheer political innocence. But I have shown that you have descended to demagogy, and I shall never tire of repeating that demagogues are the worst enemies of the working class. They are the worst enemies of the working class because they arouse bad instincts in the crowd, because the ignorant worker is unable to recognise his enemies in men who represent themselves, and sometimes sincerely represent themselves, to be his friends. They are the worst enemies of the working class, because in this period of doubt and hesitation, when our movement is only just beginning to take shape, nothing is easier than to employ demagogic methods to side-track the crowd, which can realise its mistake only by bitter experience. That is why Russian Social-Democrats at the present time must declare determined opposition to *Svoboda* and the *Rabocheye Dyelo* which have sunk to the level of demagogy. We shall return to this subject again.*

* For the moment we shall observe merely that our remarks on "pushing on from outside" and the other views on organisation expressed by *Svoboda* apply equally to *all* the Economists including the adherents of *Rabocheye Dyelo*, for they have either themselves preached and defended such views on organisation, or have allowed themselves to be led astray by them.

"A dozen wise men can be more easily caught than a hundred fools!" This wonderful truth (which the hundred fools will applaud) appears obvious only because in the very midst of the argument you have skipped from one question to another. You began by talking, and continued to talk, of catching a "committee," of catching an "organisation," and now you skip to the question of getting hold of the "roots" of the movement in the "depths." The fact is, of course, that our movement cannot be caught precisely because it has hundreds and hundreds of thousands of roots deep down among the masses, but that is not the point we are discussing. As far as "roots in the depths" are concerned, we cannot be "caught" even now, in spite of all our primitiveness; but, we all complain, and cannot but complain, of the ease with which the *organisations* can be caught, with the result that it is impossible to maintain continuity in the movement. If you agree to discuss the question of catching the *organisations,* and to stick to that question, then I assert that it is far more difficult to catch ten wise men than it is to catch a hundred fools. And this premise I shall defend no matter how much you instigate the crowd against me for my "anti-democratic" views, etc. As I have already said, by "wise men," in connection with organisation, I mean *professional revolutionists,* irrespective of whether they are students or working men. I assert: 1. That no movement can be durable without a stable organisation of leaders to maintain continuity; 2. that the more widely the masses are drawn into the struggle and form the basis of the movement, the more necessary is it to have such an organisation and the more stable must it be (for it is much easier then for demagogues to side-track the more backward sections of the masses); 3. that the organisation must consist chiefly of persons engaged in revolution as a profession; 4. that in a country with a despotic government, the more we *restrict* the membership of this organisation to persons who are engaged in revolution as a profession and who have been professionally trained in the art of combating the political police, the more difficult will it be to catch the organisation; and 5. the *wider* will be the circle of men and women of the working class or of other classes of society able to join the movement and perform active work in it.

I invite our Economists, terrorists and "Economists-terrorists" *

* This latter term is perhaps more applicable to *Svoboda* than the former, for in an article entitled "The Regeneration of Revolutionism" it defends

to confute these premises. At the moment, I shall deal only with the last two points. The question as to whether it is easier to catch "a dozen wise men" or "a hundred fools," in the last analysis, amounts to the question we have considered above, namely, whether it is possible to have a mass *organisation* when the maintenance of strict secrecy is essential. We can never give a mass organisation that degree of secrecy which is essential for the persistent and continuous struggle against the government. But to concentrate all secret functions in the hands of as small a number of professional revolutionists as possible, does not mean that the latter will "do the thinking for all" and that the crowd will not take an active part in the movement. On the contrary, the crowd will advance from its ranks increasing numbers of professional revolutionists, for it will know that it is not enough for a few students and workingmen waging economic war to gather together and form a "committee," but that professional revolutionists must be trained for years; the crowd will "think" not of primitive ways but of training professional revolutionists. The centralisation of the secret functions of the *organisation* does not mean the concentration of all the functions of the *movement*. The active participation of the greatest masses in the dissemination of illegal literature will not diminish because a dozen professional revolutionists concentrate in their hands the secret part of the work; on the contrary, it will *increase tenfold*. Only in this way will the reading of illegal literature, the contribution to illegal literature, and to some extent even the distribution of illegal literature *almost cease to be secret work*, for the police will soon come to realise the folly and futility of setting the whole judicial and administrative machine into motion to intercept every copy of a publication that is being broadcast in thousands. This applies not only to the press, but to every function of the movement, even to demonstrations. The active and wide-

terrorism, while in the article at present under review it defends Economism. One might say of *Svoboda* that—"It would if it could, but it can't." Its wishes and intentions are excellent—but the result is utter confusion; and this is chiefly due to the fact that while *Svoboda* advocates continuity of organisation, it refuses to recognise the continuity of revolutionary thought and of Social-Democratic theory. It wants to revive the professional revolutionist ("The Regeneration of Revolutionism"), and to that end proposes, firstly, excitative terrorism, and secondly, "The organisation of the average worker," because he will be less likely to be "pushed on from outside." In other words, it proposes to pull the house down to use the timbers for warming it.

spread participation of the masses will not suffer; on the contrary, it will benefit by the fact that a "dozen" experienced revolutionists, no less professionally trained than the police, will concentrate all the secret side of the work in their hands—prepare leaflets, work out approximate plans and appoint bodies of leaders for each town district, for each factory district, and for each educational institution (I know that exception will be taken to my "undemocratic" views, but I shall reply to this altogether unintelligent objection later on). The centralisation of the more secret functions in an organisation of revolutionists will not diminish, but rather increase the extent and the quality of the activity of a large number of other organisations intended for wide membership and which, therefore, can be as loose and as public as possible, for example, trade unions, workers' circles for self-education, and the reading of illegal literature, and Socialist, and also democratic, circles for *all other sections of the population*, etc., etc. We must have *as large a number as possible* of such organisations having the widest possible variety of functions, but it is absurd and dangerous to *confuse these with organisations of revolutionists*, to erase the line of demarcation between them, to dim still more the already incredibly hazy appreciation by the masses that to "serve" the mass movement we must have people who will devote themselves exclusively to Social-Democratic activities, and that such people must *train* themselves patiently and steadfastly to be professional revolutionists.

Aye, this consciousness has become incredibly dim. The most grievous sin we have committed in regard to organisation is that *by our primitiveness we have lowered the prestige of revolutionists in Russia.* A man who is weak and vacillating on theoretical questions, who has a narrow outlook, who makes excuses for his own slackness on the ground that the masses are awakening spontaneously, who resembles a trade-union secretary more than a people's tribune, who is unable to conceive a broad and bold plan, who is incapable of inspiring even his enemies with respect for himself, and who is inexperienced and clumsy in his own professional art— the art of combating the political police—such a man is not a revolutionist but a hopeless amateur!

Let no active worker take offence at these frank remarks, for as far as insufficient training is concerned, I apply them first and foremost to myself. I used to work in a circle that set itself a great and all-embracing task: and every member of that circle suffered to the point of torture from the realisation that we were proving ourselves to be amateurs at a moment in history when we might have been able to say—paraphrasing a well-known epigram: "Give us an organisation of revolutionists, and we shall overturn the whole of Russia!" And the more I recall the burning sense of shame I then experienced, the more bitter are my feelings towards those pseudo-Social-Democrats whose teachings bring disgrace on the calling of a revolutionist, who fail to understand that our task is not to degrade the revolutionist to the level of an amateur, but to *exalt* the amateur to the level of a revolutionist.

D. The Scope of Organisational Work

We have already heard from B-v about "the lack of revolutionary forces fit for action which is felt not only in St. Petersburg, but over the whole of Russia." No one, we suppose, will dispute this fact. But the question is, how is it to be explained? B-v writes:

> We shall not enter in detail into the historical causes of this phenomenon; we shall state merely that a society demoralised by prolonged political reaction and split by past and present economic changes, advances from its own ranks *an extremely small number of persons fit for revolutionary work;* that the working class does of course advance from its own ranks revolutionary workers who to some extent pass into the ranks of the illegal organisations, but the number of such revolutionists are inadequate to meet the requirements of the times. This is more particularly the case because the workers engaged for eleven and a half hours a day in the factory may perhaps be able to fulfil mainly the functions of an agitator; but propaganda and organisation, delivery and reproduction of illegal literature, issuing leaflets, etc., are duties which must necessarily fall mainly upon the shoulders of an extremely small intelligent force. [*Rabocheye Dyelo*, No. 6, pp. 38-39.]

There are many points in the above upon which we disagree with B-v, particularly with those points we have emphasised, and which most strikingly reveal that, although suffering (as every practical worker who thinks over the position would be) from our primitive methods, B-v cannot, because he is so ground down by Economism, find the way out of this intolerable situation. It is not true to say that society advances from its ranks few persons fit for "work." It advances *very many* but we are unable to make use of them all. The critical, transitional state of our movement in this connection may be formulated as follows: *There are no people—yet there are enormous numbers of people.* There are enormous numbers of people, because the working class and the most diverse strata of society, year after year, advance from their ranks an increasing number of discontented people who desire to protest, who are ready to render effective aid in the fight against absolutism, the intolerableness of which is not yet recognised by all, but is nevertheless more and more acutely sensed by increasing masses of the people. At the same time we have no people, because we have no political leaders, we have no talented organisers capable of organising extensive and at the same time uniform and harmonious work that would give employment to all forces, even the most inconsiderable. "The growth and development of revolutionary organisations" not only lag behind the growth of the labour movement, which even B-v admits, but also behind the general democratic movement among all strata of the people (in passing, probably B-v would now admit this supplement to his conclusion). The scope of revolutionary work is too narrow compared with the breadth of the spontaneous basis of the movement. It is too hemmed in by the wretched theory about the "economic struggle against the employers and the government." And yet, at the present time, not only Social-Democratic political agitators, but also Social-Democratic organisers must "go among all classes of the population." *

There is hardly a single practical worker, we think, who would have any doubt about the ability of Social-Democrats to distribute the thousand-and-one minute functions of their organisational work among the various representatives of the most varied classes. Lack of specialisation is one of our most serious technical defects, about which B-v justly and bitterly complains. The smaller each separate "operation" in our common cause will be, the more people we shall find capable of carrying out such operations (who, in the majority of cases, are not capable of becoming professional revolutionists), the more difficult will it be for the police to "catch" all these "detail workers," and the more difficult will it be for them to frame up, out of an arrest for some petty affair, a "case" that would justify the government's expenditure on the "secret service." As for the number ready to help us, we have already in the previous chapter referred to the gigantic change that has taken place in this respect

* For example, in military circles an undoubted revival of the democratic spirit has recently been observed, partly as a consequence of the frequent street fights that now take place against "enemies" like workers and students. And as soon as our available forces permit, we must without fail devote serious attention to propaganda and agitation among soldiers and officers, and to creating "military organisations" affiliated to our party.

in the last five years or so. On the other hand, in order to unite all these tiny fractions into one whole, in order to avoid breaking the movement up into fragments, in breaking up functions, and in order to imbue those who carry out these minute functions with the conviction of the necessity for and importance of their work, without which they will never do the work,* it is necessary to have an organisation of tried revolutionists. If we had such an organisation, the more secret it would be, the stronger and more widespread would be the confidence of the masses in the party, and, as we know, in time of war, it is not only of great importance to imbue one's own adherents with confidence in the strength of one's army, but also the enemy and all *neutral* elements; friendly neutrality may sometimes decide the outcome of the battle. If such an organisation existed on a firm theoretical basis, and possessed a Social-Democratic journal, we would have no reason to fear that the movement will be diverted from its path by the numerous "outside" elements that will be attracted to it. (On the contrary, it is precisely at the present time, when primitive methods prevail among us, that many Social-Democrats are observed to gravitate towards the *Credo*, imagining that they alone are Social-Democrats.) In a word, specialisation necessarily presupposes centralisation, and in its turn imperatively calls for it.

But B-v himself, who has so excellently described the necessity for specialisation, underestimates its importance, in our opinion, in the second part of the argument that we have quoted. The number

* I recall the story a comrade related to me of a factory inspector, who, desiring to help, and in fact did help, Social-Democracy, bitterly complained that he did not know whether the "information" he sent reached the proper revolutionary quarter; he did not know how much his help was really required, and what possibilities there were for utilising his small services. Every practical worker, of course, knows of more than one case similar to this, of our primitiveness depriving us of allies. And these services, each "small" in itself, but incalculable taken together, could be rendered to us by office employees and officials, not only in factories, but in the postal service, on the railways, in the Customs, among the nobility, among the clergy, and *every other* walk of life, including even the police service and the Court! Had we a real party, a real militant organisation of revolutionists, we would not put the question bluntly to every one of these "abettors," we would not hasten in every single case to bring them right into the very heart of our "illegality," but, on the contrary, we would husband them very carefully and would train people especially for such functions, bearing in mind that many students could be of much greater service to the party as "abettors" —officials—than as "short-term" revolutionists. But, I repeat, only an organisation that is already firmly established and has no lack of active forces would have the right to apply such tactics.

of working-class revolutionists is inadequate, he says. This is absolutely true, and once again we emphasise that the "valuable communication of a close observer" fully confirms our view of the causes of the present crisis in Social-Democracy, and, consequently, confirms our view of the means for removing these causes. Not only revolutionists, in general, but even working-class revolutionists lag behind the spontaneous awakening of the working masses. And this *fact* most strikingly confirms, even from the "practical" point-of-view, not only the absurdity but even the *political reaction-ariness* of the "pedagogics" to which we are so often treated when discussing our duties to the workers. This fact proves that our very first and most imperative duty is to help to train working-class revolutionists who will be on the same level *in regard to party activity* as intellectual revolutionists (we emphasise the words "in regard to party activity," because although it is necessary, it is not so easy and not so imperative to bring the workers up to the level of intellectuals in other respects). Therefore, attention must be devoted *principally* to the task of *raising* the workers to the level of revolutionists, but without, in doing so, necessarily *degrading* ourselves to the level of the "labouring masses," as the Economists wish to do, or necessarily to the level of the average worker, as *Svoboda* desires to do (and by this, raises itself to the second grade of Economists "pedagogics"). I am far from denying the necessity for popular literature for the workers, and especially popular (but, of course, not vulgar) literature for the especially backward workers. But what annoys me is that pedagogics are confused with questions of politics and organisation. You, gentlemen, who talk so much about the "average worker," as a matter of fact, rather insult the workers by your desire to *talk down* to them, to stoop to them when discussing labour politics or labour organisation. Talk about serious things in a serious manner; leave pedagogics to the pedagogues, and not to politicians and to organisers! Are there not advanced people, "average people," and "masses," among the intelligentsia? Does not every one recognise that popular literature is required for the intelligentsia and is not such literature written? Just imagine some one, in an article on organising college or high-school students, repeating over and over again, as if he had made a new discovery, that first of all we must have an organisation of "average students." The author of such an article would rightly be laughed at. He will be told: Give us an organisation idea, if you have one, and we ourselves will settle the question as to which of us are "average," as to who is higher and who is lower. But if you have no organisational ideas *of your own,* then all your chatter about "masses" and "average" is just simply boring. Try to understand that these questions about "politics" and "organisation" are so serious in themselves that they cannot be dealt with in any other but a serious way: We can and must *educate* workers (and university and high-school students) so as to enable them to understand us *when we speak to them* about these questions; and when you come to talk about these questions to us give us real replies to them, do not fall back on the "average," or on the "masses"; don't evade them by quoting adages or mere phrases.*

In order to be fully prepared for his task, the working-class revolutionist must also become a professional revolutionist. Hence B-v is wrong when he says that as the worker is engaged for 11½ hours a day in the factory, therefore the brunt of all the other revolutionary functions (apart from agitation) *"must necessarily fall mainly upon the shoulders of an extremely small intellectual force."* It need not "necessarily" be so. It is so because we are backward, because we do not recognise our duty to assist every capable worker to become a *professional* agitator, organiser, propagandist, literature distributor, etc., etc. In this respect, we waste our strength in a positively shameful manner; we lack the ability to husband that which requires to be so carefully tended in order that it may grow. Look at the Germans: they have a hundred times more forces than we have. But they understand perfectly well that the "average" does not too frequently promote really capable agitators, etc., from its ranks. Hence, immediately they get a capable workingman, they try to place him in such conditions as will enable him to develop and apply his abilities to the utmost: he is made a professional agitator, he is encouraged to widen the field of his activity, to spread it from one factory to the whole of his trade, from one locality to the whole country. He acquires experi-

* *Svoboda* No. 1, p. 66, articles on "Organisation": "The heavy tread of the army of labour will re-inforce all the demands that will be advanced by Russian Labour"—Labour with a capital L, of course. And this very author exclaims: "I am not in the least hostile towards the intelligentsia, but" [This is the very word *but* that Shchedrin translated as meaning: The ears never grow higher than the forehead!] "but I get frightfully annoyed when a man comes to me and eloquently appeals to be accepted for his [his?] beauty and virtues" [p. 62]. Yes. This "always frightfully annoys" me too.

ence and dexterity in his profession, his outlook becomes wider, his knowledge increases, he observes the prominent political leaders from other localities and other parties, he strives to rise to their level and combine within himself the knowledge of working-class environment and freshness of Socialist convictions with professional skill, without which the proletariat *cannot* carry on a stubborn struggle with the excellently trained enemy. Only in this way can men of the stamp of Bebel and Auer be promoted from the ranks of the working class. But what takes place very largely automatically in a politically free country, must in Russia be done deliberately and systematically by our organisations. A workingman who is at all talented and "promising," *must not be left* to work eleven hours a day in a factory. We must arrange that he be maintained by the party, that he may in due time go underground, that he change the place of his activity, otherwise he will not enlarge his experience, he will not widen his outlook, and will not be able to stay in the fight against the gendarmes for several years. As the spontaneous rise of the labouring masses becomes wider and deeper, it not only promotes from its ranks an increasing number of talented agitators, but also of talented organisers, propagandists, and "practical workers" in the best sense of the term (of whom there are so few among our intelligentsia). In the majority of cases, the latter are somewhat careless and sluggish in their habits (so characteristic of Russians). When we shall have detachments of specially trained working-class revolutionists who have gone through long years of preparation (and, of course, revolutionists "of all arms") no political police in the world will be able to contend against them, for these detachments will consist of men absolutely devoted and loyal to the revolution, and will themselves enjoy the absolute confidence and devotion of the broad masses of the workers. The *sin* we commit is that we do not sufficiently "stimulate" the workers to take this path, "common" to them and to the "intellectuals," of professional revolutionary training, and that we too frequently drag them back by our silly speeches about what "can be understood" by the masses of the workers, by the "average workers," etc.

In this, as in other cases, the narrowness of our field of organisational work is without a doubt inherently due (although the overwhelming majority of the Economists and the novices in practical work refuse to recognise it) to the fact that we restrict our theories and our political tasks to a narrow field. Subservience to spontaneity seems to inspire a fear to take even one step away from what "can be understood" by the masses, a fear to rise too high above mere subservience to the immediate requirements of the masses. Have no fear, gentlemen! Remember that we stand so low on the plane of organisation, that the very idea that we could rise *too high* is absurd!

E. "Conspirative" Organisation and "Democracy"

There are many people among us who are so sensitive to the "voice of life" that they fear that voice more than anything in the world, and accuse those, who adhere to the views here expounded, of Narodovolism,* of failing to understand "democracy," etc. We must deal with these accusations, which, of course, have been echoed by *Rabocheye Dyelo*.

The writer of these lines knows very well that the St. Petersburg Economists accused the *Rabochaya Gazeta* of being Narodovolist (which is quite understandable when one compares it with *Rabochaya Mysl*). We were not in the least surprised, therefore, when, soon after the appearance of *Iskra*, a comrade informed us that the Social-Democrats in the town of X describe *Iskra* as a Narodovolist journal. We, of course, were flattered by this accusation, because the Economists would charge every real Social-Democrat with being a Narodovolist. These accusations are called forth by a two-fold misunderstanding. Firstly, the history of the revolutionary movement is so little understood among us that the very idea of a militant centralised organisation which declares a determined war upon tsarism is described as Narodovolist. But the magnificent organisation that the revolutionists had in the seventies and which should serve us all as a model, was not formed by the Narodovolists, but by the adherents of Zemlya i Volya, who split up into Chernoperedeltsi [Black Redistributionists—*i. e.*, of the land.—*Ed.*] and Narodovolists. Consequently, to regard a militant revolutionary organisation as something specifically Narodovolist is absurd both historically and logically, because no revolutionary tendency, if it seriously thinks of fighting, can dispense with such an organisation. But the mistake the Narodovolists committed was not that they strove to recruit to their organisation *all* the discontented, and to hurl this organisation into the battle against the

* Adherents of Narodnaya Volya, the People's Will Party.—*Ed.*

autocracy; on the contrary, that was their great historical merit. Their mistake was that they relied on a theory which in substance was not a revolutionary theory at all, and they either did not know how, or circumstances did not permit them, to link up their movement inseparably with the class struggle that went on within developing capitalist society. And only a gross failure to understand Marxism (or an "understanding" of it in the spirit of Struveism) could give rise to the opinion that the rise of a mass, spontaneous labour movement *relieves* us of the duty of creating as good an organisation of revolutionists as Zemlya i Volya had in its time, and even a better one. On the contrary, this movement *imposes* this duty upon us, because the spontaneous struggle of the proletariat will not become a genuine "class struggle" until it is led by a strong organisation of revolutionists.

Secondly, many, including apparently B. Krichevsky [*Rabocheye Dyelo*, No. 10, p. 18] misunderstand the polemics that Social-Democrats have always waged against the "conspiratorial" view on the political struggle. We have always protested, and will, of course, continue to protest against *restricting* the political struggle to conspiracies.* But this does not of course mean that we deny the necessity of a strong revolutionary organisation. And in the pamphlet mentioned in the footnote below, after the polemics against reducing the political struggle to a conspiracy, a description is given (as a Social-Democratic ideal) of an organisation so strong as to be able to resort to "rebellion" and to "every other form of attack," ** in order to "deliver a smashing blow against absolutism." The *form* a strong revolutionary organisation like that may take in an autocratic country may be described as a "conspirative" organ-

* *Cf. The Tasks of Russian Social-Democrats*, p. 21. Polemics against P. L. Lavrov. [See V. I. Lenin, *Collected Works*, Vol. II.—*Ed.*]

** *Tasks of Russian Social-Democrats*, p. 23. [V. I. Lenin, *Collected Works*, Vol. II.—*Ed.*] But we shall give another illustration of the fact that *Rabocheye Dyelo* either does not understand what it is talking about, or changes its views "with every change in the wind." In No. 1 of *Rabocheye Dyelo*, we find the following passage in italics: "*The views expressed in this pamphlet coincide entirely with the editorial programme of Rabocheye Dyelo* [p. 142]. Is that so, indeed? Does the view that the mass movement must not be set the primary task of overthrowing the autocracy coincide with the views expressed in the pamphlet, *The Tasks of Russian Social-Democrats?* Do the theories about "the economic struggle against the employers and the government," and the theory of stages, coincide with the views expressed in that pamphlet? We leave it to the reader to judge as to whether an organ which understands the meaning of "coincidence" in this peculiar manner can have firm principles.

isation, because the French word *"conspiration"* means in Russian "conspiracy," and we must have the utmost conspiracy for an organisation like that.* Secrecy is such a necessary condition for such an organisation that all the other conditions (number and selection of members, functions, etc.) must all be subordinated to it. It would be extremely naïve indeed, therefore, to fear the accusation that we Social-Democrats desire to create a conspirative organisation. Such an accusation would be as flattering to every opponent of Economism as the accusation of being followers of Narodovolism would be.

Against us it is argued: Such a powerful and strictly secret organisation, which concentrates in its hands all the threads of secret activities, an organisation which of necessity must be a centralised organisation, may too easily throw itself into a premature attack, may thoughtlessly intensify the movement before political discontent, the ferment and anger of the working class, etc., are sufficiently ripe for it. To this we reply: Speaking abstractly, it cannot be denied, of course, that a militant organisation *may* thoughtlessly commence a battle, which *may* end in defeat, which might have been avoided under other circumstances. But we cannot confine ourselves to abstract reasoning on such a question, because every battle bears within itself the abstract possibility of defeat, and there is no other way of *reducing this possibility to a minimum* than by organised preparation for battle. If, however, we base our argument on the concrete conditions prevailing in Russia at the present time, we must come to the positive conclusion that a strong revolutionary organisation is absolutely necessary precisely for the purpose of giving firmness to the movement, and of *safeguarding* it against the possibility of its making premature attacks. It is precisely at the present time, when no such organisation exists yet, and when the revolutionary movement is rapidly and spontaneously growing, that we *already observe* two opposite extremes (which, as is to be expected, "meet") *i. e.*, absolutely unsound Economism and the preaching of moderation, and equally unsound "excitative

* The Russian word for "conspiracy" is *zagovor*, which means "conspiracy" or "plot." But the word *conspiratsiya*, "conspiracy," in Russian revolutionary literature usually means "secrecy." Hence, a conspirative organisation would be a secret organisation, but would not necessarily engage in plots. Except in the above case, when it was important to bring out the play of words, the word *"conspiratsiya"* has been rendered throughout the text as "secrecy," and the word "conspirative" was used only where the word *zagovor* has been used in the text, as in the sub-title of this section.—*Ed.*

127

terror," which strives artificially to "call forth symptoms of its end in a movement that is developing and becoming strong, but which is as yet nearer to its beginning than to its end" [V. Zasulich, in *Zarya*, Nos. 2-3, p. 353]. And the example of *Rabocheye Dyelo* shows that *there are already* Social-Democrats who give way to both these extremes. This is not surprising because, apart from other reasons, the "economic struggle against the employers and the government" *can never* satisfy revolutionists, and because opposite extremes will always arise here and there. Only a centralised, militant organisation, that consistently carries out a Social-Democratic policy, that satisfies, so to speak, all revolutionary instincts and strivings, can safeguard the movement against making thoughtless attacks and prepare it for attacks that hold out the promise of success.

It is further argued against us that the views on organisation here expounded contradict the "principles of democracy." Now while the first mentioned accusation was of purely Russian origin, this one is of *purely foreign* origin. And only an organisation abroad (the League of Russian Social-Democrats) would be capable of giving its editorial board instructions like the following:

Principles of Organisation. In order to secure the successful development and unification of Social-Democracy, broad democratic principles of party organisation must be emphasised, developed and fought for; and this is particularly necessary in view of the anti-democratic tendencies that have become revealed in the ranks of our party. [*Two Congresses*, p. 18.]

We shall see how *Rabocheye Dyelo* fights against *Iskra's* "anti-democratic tendencies" in the next chapter. Here we shall examine more closely the "principle" that the Economists advance. Every one will probably agree that "broad principles of democracy" presupposes the two following conditions: first, full publicity and second, election to all functions. It would be absurd to speak about democracy without publicity, that is a publicity that extends beyond the circle of the membership of the organisation. We call the German Socialist Party a democratic organisation because all it does is done publicly; even its party congresses are held in public. But no one would call an organisation that is hidden from every one but its members by a veil of secrecy, a democratic organisation. What is the use of advancing "*broad* principles of democracy" when the fundamental condition for this principle *cannot be fulfilled* by a secret organisation. "Broad principles" turns out to be a resonant, but hollow phrase. More than that, this phrase proves that the urgent tasks in regard to organisation are totally misunderstood. Every one knows how great is the lack of secrecy among the "broad" masses of revolutionists. We have heard the bitter complaints of B-v on this score, and his absolutely just demand for a "strict selection of members" [*Rabocheye Dyelo*, No. 6, p. 42]. And yet people who boast about their "sensitiveness to life" come forward in a situation like this and *urge* that strict secrecy and a strict (and therefore more restricted) selection of members is unnecessary, and that what is necessary are—"*broad* principles of democracy"! This is what we call being absolutely wide of the mark.

Nor is the situation with regard to the second attribute of democracy, namely, the principle of election, any better. In politically free countries, this condition is taken for granted. "Membership of the party is open to those who accept the principles of the party programme, and render all the support they can to the party"— says paragraph 1 of the rules of the German Social-Democratic Party. And as the political arena is as open to the public view as is the stage in a theatre, this acceptance or non-acceptance, support or opposition is announced to all in the press and at public meetings. Every one knows that a certain political worker commenced in a certain way, passed through a certain evolution, behaved in difficult periods in a certain way; every one knows all his qualities, and consequently, knowing all the facts of the case, *every party member can decide for himself whether or not to elect this person for a certain party office.* The general control (in the literal sense of the term) that the party exercises over every act this person commits on the political field brings into being an automatically operating mechanism which brings about what in biology is called "survival of the fittest." "Natural selection," full publicity, the principle of election and general control provide the guarantee that, in the last analysis, every political worker will be "in his proper place," will do the work for which he is best fitted, will feel the effects of his mistakes on himself, and prove before all the world his ability to recognise mistakes and to avoid them.

Try to put this picture in the frame of our autocracy! Is it possible in Russia for all those "who accept the principles of the party programme and render it all the support they can," to control every action of the revolutionist working in secret? Is it possible for all the revolutionists to elect one of their number to any particular office when, in the very interests of the work, he *must conceal his identity* from nine out of ten of these "all"? Ponder a little over the real meaning of the high-sounding phrases that *Rabocheye Dyelo* gives utterance to, and you will realise that "broad democracy" in party organisation, amidst the gloom of autocracy and the domination of the gendarmes, is nothing more than a *useless and harmful toy.* It is a useless toy, because as a matter of fact, no revolutionary organisation has ever practiced *broad* democracy, nor could it, however much it desired to do so. It is a harmful toy, because any attempt to practice the "broad principles of democracy" will simply facilitate the work of the police in making big raids, it will perpetuate the prevailing primitiveness, divert the thoughts of the practical workers from the serious and imperative task of training themselves to become professional revolutionists to that of drawing up detailed "paper" rules for election systems. Only abroad, where very often people who have no opportunity of doing real live work gather together, can the "game of democracy" be played here and there, especially in small groups.

In order to show how ugly *Rabocheye Dyelo's* favourite trick is of advancing the plausible "principle" of democracy in revolutionary affairs, we shall again call a witness. This witness, E. Serebryakov, the editor of the London magazine, *Nakanunye* [*On the Eve*] has a tenderness for *Rabocheye Dyelo*, and is filled with hatred against Plekhanov and the Plekhanovists. In articles that it published on the split in the League of Russian Social-Democrats Abroad, *Nakanunye* definitely took the side of *Rabocheye Dyelo*, and poured a stream of atrocious abuse upon Plekhanov. But this only makes this witness all the more valuable for us on this question. In No. 7 of *Nakanunye* [July, 1899], in an article, entitled, "The Manifesto of the Self-Emancipation of the Workers' Group," E. Serebryakov argues that it was "indecent" to talk about such things as "self-deception, priority, and so-called Areopagus in the serious revolutionary movement," and *inter alia* wrote:

Myshkin, Rogachev, Zhelyabov, Mikhailov, Perovskaya, Figner, and others never regarded themselves as leaders, and no one ever elected or appointed them as such, although as a matter of fact, they were leaders because both in the propaganda period, as well as in the period of the fight against the government, they took the brunt of the work upon themselves, they went into the most dangerous places and their activities were the most fruitful. Priority came to them not because they wished it, but because the comrades surrounding them had confidence in their wisdom, their energy and loyalty. To be afraid of some kind of Areopagus [if it is not feared, then why write about it?] that would arbitrarily govern the movement is far too naïve. Who would obey it?

We ask the reader in what way does "Areopagus" differ from "anti-democratic tendencies"? And is it not evident that *Rabocheye Dyelo's* "plausible" organisational principles are equally naïve and indecent; naïve, because no one would obey "Areopagus," or people with "anti-democratic tendencies," if "the comrades surrounding them had no confidence in their wisdom, energy and loyalty"; indecent, because it is a demagogic sally calculated to play on the conceit of some, on the ignorance of the actual state of our movement on the part of others, and the lack of training and ignorance of the history of the revolutionary movement of still others. The only serious organisational principle the active workers of our movement can accept is: Strict secrecy, strict selection of members, and the training of professional revolutionists. If we possessed these qualities, "democracy" and something even more would be guaranteed to us, namely: Complete, comradely, mutual confidence among revolutionists. And this something more is absolutely essential for us because, in Russia, it is useless to think that democratic control can serve as a substitute for it. It would be a great mistake to believe that because it is impossible to establish real "democratic" control, the members of the revolutionary organisation will remain altogether uncontrolled. They have not the time to think about the toy forms of democracy (democracy within a close and compact body enjoying the complete mutual confidence of the comrades), but they have a lively sense of their *responsibility*, because they know from experience that an organisation of real revolutionists will stop at nothing to rid itself of an undesirable member. Moreover, there is a very well-developed public opinion in Russian (and international) revolutionary circles which has a long history behind it, and which sternly and ruthlessly punishes every departure from the duties of comradeship (and does not "democracy," real and not toy democracy, represent a part of the conception of comradeship?). Take all this into consideration and you will realise that all the talk and resolutions that come from abroad about "anti-democratic tendencies" has a nasty odour of the playing at generals that goes on there.

It must be observed also that the other source of this talk, *i. e.*, naïveté, is also fostered by a confusion of ideas concerning the meaning of democracy. In Mr. and Mrs. Webb's book on trade unionism,* there is an interesting section on "Primitive Democracy." In this section, the authors relate how, in the first period of existence of their unions, the British workers thought that in the interests of democracy all the members must take part in the work of managing the unions; not only were all questions decided by the votes of all the members, but all the official duties were fulfilled by all the members in turn. A long period of historical experience was required to teach these workers how absurd such a conception of democracy was and to make them understand the necessity for representative institutions on the one hand, and of full-time professional officials on the other. Only after a number of cases of financial bankruptcy of trade unions occurred did the workers realise that rates of benefit cannot be decided merely by a democratic vote, but must be based on the advice of insurance experts. Let us take also Kautsky's book, *Der Parlamentarismus, die Volksgesetzgebung und die Sozialdemokratie.* There you will find that the conclusion drawn by the Marxian theoretician coincides with the lessons learned from many years of experience by the workers who organised "spontaneously." Kautsky strongly protests against Rittinghausen's primitive conception of democracy; he ridicules those who in the name of democracy demand even that "popular newspapers shall be directly edited by the people"; he shows the necessity for *professional* journalists, parliamentarians, etc., and for the Social-Democratic leadership of the proletarian class struggle; he attacks the "Socialism of Anarchists and *litterateurs,*" who in their "striving after effect" proclaim the principle that laws should be passed directly by the whole people, completely failing to understand that in modern society this principle can have only a relative application.

Those who have carried on practical work in our movement know how widespread is the "primitive" conception of democracy among the masses of the students and workers. It is not surprising that this conception permeates rules of organisation and literature. The Economists of the Bernstein persuasion included in their rules the following: "§ 10. All affairs affecting the interests of the whole of the union organisation shall be decided by a majority vote of all its members." The Economists of the terrorist persuasion re-

* *The History of Trade Unionism.*

peat after them: "The decisions of the committee must be circulated among all the circles and become effective only after this has been done" [*Svoboda*, No. 1, p. 67]. Observe that this proposal for a widely applied referendum is advanced *in addition* to the demand that *the whole of* the organisation be organised on an elective basis! We would not, of course, on this account condemn practical workers who have had too few opportunities for studying the theory and practice of real democratic organisation. But when *Rabocheye Dyelo*, which claims to play a leading rôle, confines itself, under such conditions, to resolutions about broad democratic principles, how else can it be described than as a "striving after effect"?

F. Local and All-Russian Work

Although the objections raised against the plan for an organisation outlined here on the grounds of its undemocratic and conspirative character are totally unsound, nevertheless a question still remains that is frequently put and which deserves detailed examination. This is the question about the relations between local work and All-Russian work. Fears are expressed that this would lead to the formation of a centralised organisation, and that national work would be over-stressed at the expense of local work; that this would damage the movement, would weaken our contacts with the masses of the workers, and would weaken local agitation generally. To these fears we reply that our movement in the past few years has suffered precisely from the fact that the local workers have been too absorbed in local work. Hence it is absolutely necessary to somewhat shift the weight of the work from local work to national work. This would not weaken, on the contrary, it would strengthen our ties and our local agitation. Take the question of central and local journals. I would ask the reader not to forget that we cite the publication of journals only as *an example,* illustrating an immeasurably broader and more widespread revolutionary activity.

In the first period of the mass movement (1896-1898), an attempt is made by local party workers to publish an All-Russian journal, the *Rabochaya Gazeta*. In the next period (1898-1900), the movement makes enormous strides, but the attention of the leaders is wholly absorbed by local publications. If we add up all the local journals that were published, we shall find that on the average one paper per month was published.* Does not this illustrate our primitive ways? Does this not clearly show that our revolutionary organisation lags behind the spontaneous growth of the movement? If *the same number* of issues had been published, not by scattered local groups, but by a single organisation, we would not only have saved an enormous amount of effort, but we would have secured immeasurably greater stability and continuity in our work. This simple calculation is very frequently lost sight of by those practical workers who work *actively*, almost exclusively, on local publications (unfortunately this is the case even now in the overwhelming majority of cases) as well as by the publicists who display an astonishing Quixotism on this question. The practical workers usually rest content with the argument that "it is difficult" for local workers to engage in the organisation of an All-Russian newspaper, and that local newspapers are better than no newspapers at all.** The latter argument is, of course, perfectly just, and we shall not be behind any practical worker in our recognition of the enormous importance and usefulness of local newspapers *in general*. But this is not the point. The point is, Can we rid ourselves of the state of diffusion and primitiveness that is so strikingly expressed in the thirty numbers of local newspapers published throughout the whole of Russia in the course of two-and-a-half years? Do not restrict yourselves to indisputable but too general statements about the usefulness of local newspapers generally; have the courage also openly to recognise their defects as have been revealed by the experience of two-and-a-half years. This experience has shown that under the conditions in which we work, these local newspapers prove, in the majority of cases, to be unstable in their principles, lacking in political significance, extremely costly in regard to expenditure of revolutionary effort, and totally unsatisfactory from a technical point of view (I have in mind, of course, not the technique of printing them, but the frequency and regularity of publication). These defects are not accidental; they are the inevitable result of the diffusion which on the one hand ex-

---

* See *Report to the Paris Congress*, p. 14. "Since that time (1897) to the spring of 1900, thirty issues of various papers were published in various places. . . . On average, over one number per month was published.

** This difficulty is more apparent than real. As a matter of fact, *there is not a single* local circle that lacks the opportunity of taking up some function or other in connection with All-Russian work. "Don't say: I can't; say: I won't."

plains the predominance of local newspapers in the period under review, and on the other hand *is fostered* by this predominance. A separate local organisation is *positively unable* to maintain stability of principles in its newspaper, and it cannot raise it to the level of a political organ; *it is unable* to collect and utilise sufficient material dealing with the whole of our political life. While, in politically free countries, it is often argued in defence of numerous local newspapers that the cost of printing by local workers is low, and that the local population can be kept more fully and quickly informed, experience has shown that in Russia this argument can be used *against* local newspapers. In Russia, local newspapers prove to be excessively costly in regard to the expenditure of revolutionary effort, and are published *rarely*, for the very simple reason that no matter how small its size, the publication of an *illegal newspaper* requires as large a secret apparatus as is required by a large enterprise, for such an apparatus cannot be run in a small, handicraft workshop. Very frequently, the primitiveness of the secret apparatus (every practical worker knows of numerous cases like this) enables the police to take advantage of the publication and distribution of one or two numbers to make *mass arrests* and to make such a clean sweep that it is necessary afterwards to build up the entire apparatus anew. A well-organised secret apparatus requires professionally well-trained revolutionists and proper division of labour, but neither of these requirements can be met by separate local organisations, no matter how strong they may be at any given moment. Not only are the general interests of our movement as a whole (consistent training of the workers in Socialist and political principles) better served by non-local newspapers, but even specifically local interests are better served. This may seem paradoxical at first sight, but it has been proved up to the hilt by the two-and-a-half years of experience to which we have already referred. Every one will agree that if all the local forces that were engaged in the publication of these thirty issues of newspapers had worked on a single newspaper, they could easily have published sixty if not a hundred numbers, and consequently, would have more fully expressed all the specifically local features of the movement. True, it is not an easy matter to attain such high degree of organisation, but we must recognise the necessity for it. Every local circle must think about it, and *work actively* to achieve it, without waiting to be pushed on from outside; and we must stop being tempted by the ease and closer proximity of a local newspaper which, as our revolutionary experience has shown, proves to a large extent to be more apparent than real.

And it is a bad service indeed those publicists render to the practical work, who, thinking they stand particularly close to the practical workers, fail to see this deceptiveness, and express the astonishingly cheap and astonishingly hollow argument: We must have local newspapers, we must have district newspapers, and we must have All-Russian newspapers. Generally speaking of course, all these are necessary, but when you undertake to solve a concrete organisational problem surely you must take time and circumstances into consideration. Is it not Quixotic on the part of *Svoboda* [No. 1, p. 68], in a special article "dealing with *the question of a newspaper*" to write: "It seems to us that every locality where any number of workingmen are collected, should have its own labour newspaper. Not a newspaper imported from somewhere or other, but its very own." If the publicist who wrote that refuses to think about the significance of his own words, then at least you, reader, think about it for him. How many scores if not hundreds of "localities where workingmen are collected in any more or less considerable number" are there in Russia, and would it not be simply perpetuating our primitive methods if indeed every local organisation set to work to publish its own newspaper? How this diffusion would facilitate the task of the gendarmes fishing out— without any considerable effort at that—the local party workers at the very beginning of their activity and preventing them from developing into real revolutionists! A reader of an All-Russian newspaper, continues the author, would *not find* descriptions of the misdeeds of the factory-owners and the "details of factory life in other towns outside his district at all interesting." But "an inhabitant of Oryol would not find it dull reading about Oryol affairs. Each time he picked up his paper he would know that some factory-owner was 'caught' and another 'exposed,' and his spirits would begin to soar" [p. 69]. Yes, yes, the spirit of the Oryolian would begin to soar, but the thoughts of our publicist also begin to soar—too high. He should have asked himself: Is it right to concern oneself entirely with defending the striving after small reforms? We are second to no one in our appreciation of the importance and necessity of factory exposures, but it must be borne in mind that we have reached a stage when St. Petersburgians find it dull reading the St.

Petersburg correspondence of the St. Petersburg *Rabochaya Mysl.* Local factory exposures have always been *and should always continue* to be made through the medium of leaflets, but we must raise the level of the *newspaper*, and not degrade it to the level of a factory leaflet. We do not require "petty" exposures for our "newspaper." We require exposures of the important, typical evils of factory life, exposures based on the most striking facts, and capable of interesting *all* workers and all leaders of the movement, capable of really enriching their knowledge, widening their outlook, and of rousing new districts and workers of new trade groups.

"Moreover, in a local newspaper, the misdeeds of the factory officials and other authorities may be seized upon immediately, and caught red-handed. In the case of a general newspaper, however, by the time the news reaches the paper, and by the time they are published, the facts will have been forgotten in the localities in which they occurred. The reader, when he gets the paper, will say: 'God knows when that happened!'" [*ibid*]. Exactly: God knows when it happened. As we know, from the source I have already quoted, during two-and-a-half years, thirty issues of newspapers were published in six cities. This, on the average, is *one issue per city per half year.* And even if our frivolous publicist *trebled* his estimate of the productivity of local work (which would be wrong in the case of an average city, because it is impossible to increase productivity to any extent by our primitive methods), we would still get only one issue every two months, *i. e.,* nothing at all like "catching them red-handed." It would be sufficient, however, to combine a score or so of local organisations, and assign active functions to their delegates in organising a general newspaper, to enable us to "seize upon," *over the whole of Russia,* not petty, but really outstanding and typical evils once every fortnight. No one who has any knowledge at all of the state of affairs in our organisations can have the slightest doubt about that. It is quite absurd to talk about an illegal newspaper capturing the enemy red-handed, that is, if we mean it seriously and not merely as a metaphor. That can only be done by an anonymous leaflet, because an incident like that can only be of interest for a matter of a day or two (take, for example, the usual, brief strikes, beatings in a factory, demonstrations, etc.).

"The workers not only live in factories, they also live in the cities," continues our author, rising from the particular to the general, with a strict consistency that would have done honour to Boris Krichevsky himself; and he refers to matters like the city councils, city hospitals, city schools, and demands that labour newspapers generally deal with these municipal affairs. This demand is an excellent one in itself, but it serves as a remarkable illustration of the empty abstraction which too frequently characterises discussions about local newspapers. First of all, if indeed newspapers appeared "in every place where any number of workers are gathered" with such detailed information on municipal affairs as *Svoboda* desires, it would, under our Russian conditions, inevitably lead to striving for small reform, to a weakening of the consciousness of the importance of an All-Russian revolutionary attack upon the tsarist autocracy, and would strengthen that extremely virile tendency, which has already become notorious by the famous remark about revolutionists who talk more about non-existent parliaments, and too little about existing city councils, and which has not been uprooted but rather temporarily suppressed. We say "inevitably," deliberately, in order to emphasise that *Svoboda* obviously does not want this but the contrary to happen. But good intentions are not enough. In order that municipal affairs may be dealt with in their proper perspective, in relation to the whole of our work, this perspective must be clearly conceived from the *very outset*; it must be firmly established, not only by argument, but by numerous examples in order that it may acquire the firmness of a *tradition*. This is far from being the case with us yet. And yet this must be done *from the very outset*, before we can even think and talk about an extensive local press.

Secondly, in order to be able to write well and interestingly about municipal affairs, one must know these questions not only from books, but from practical experience. And there are hardly any Social-Democrats *anywhere in Russia* who possess this knowledge. In order to be able to write in newspapers (not in popular pamphlets) about municipal and state affairs, one must have fresh and multifarious material collected and worked up by able journalists. And in order to be able to collect and work up such material, we must have something more than the "primitive democracy" of a primitive circle, in which everybody does everything and all entertain one another by playing at referendums. For this it is necessary to have a staff of expert writers, expert correspondents, an army of Social-Democratic reporters, that has established contacts far and wide, able to penetrate into all sorts of "state secrets" (about which the Russian government official is so puffed up, but which he so easily blabs), find its way "behind the scenes," an army of men and women whose "official duty" it must be to be ubiquitous and omniscient. And we, the party that fights against *all* economic, political, social and national oppression can and must find, collect, train, mobilise, and set into motion such an army of omniscient people—but all this has yet to be done! Not only has not a single step been taken towards this in the overwhelming majority of cases, but in many places the necessity for doing it is *not even recognised*. You will search in vain in our Social-Democratic press for lively and interesting articles, correspondence, and exposures of our diplomatic, military, ecclesiastical, municipal, financial, etc., etc., affairs and malpractices. You will find *almost nothing*, or very little, about these things.* That is why "I am always frightfully annoyed when a man comes to me and says all sorts of nice things" about the necessity for newspapers that will expose factory, municipal, and government evils "in every place where any considerable number of workers are collected!"

The predominance of the local press over the central press may be either a symptom of poverty, or a symptom of luxury. Of poverty, when the movement has not yet developed the forces for large-scale production, and continues to flounder in primitive ways and in "the petty details of factory life." Of luxury, when the movement, having *already mastered the task* of all-sided exposure and all-sided agitation, finds it necessary to publish numerous local newspapers in addition to the central organ. Let each one decide for himself as to what the predominance of local newspapers implies at the present time. I shall limit myself to a precise formulation of my own conclusion, in order to avoid misunderstanding. Hitherto the majority of our local organisations devoted their minds

* That is why even examples of exceptionally good local newspapers fully confirm our point-of-view. For example, *Yuzhny Rabochy* is an excellent newspaper, and is altogether free from instability of principles. But it was unable to provide what it desired for the local movement owing to the infrequency of its publication and to extensive police raids. What our party must do most urgently at the present time is to present the fundamental questions of the movement, and carry on wide political agitation, but this the local newspaper was unable to do. And that which it did exceptionally well, namely, publish articles about the mine-owners' congress, unemployment, etc., was not strictly local material, *it was required for the whole of Russia*, and not for the South alone. No articles like that have appeared in any of our Social-Democratic newspapers.

almost exclusively to local newspapers, and devoted almost all their activities to this work. This is unsound—the very opposite should be the case. The majority of the local organisations should devote their minds principally to the publication of an All-Russian newspaper, and devote their activities principally to this work. Until that is done, we shall never be able to establish *a single newspaper* capable to any degree of serving the movement with *all-sided* press agitation. When that is done, however, normal relations between the necessary central newspapers and the necessary local newspapers will be established automatically.

It would seem at first sight that the conclusion drawn, concerning the necessity for transferring the weight of effort from local work to All-Russian work, does not apply to the specifically economic struggle. In this struggle, the immediate enemy of the workers are individual employers or groups of employers, who are not bound by any organisation having even the remotest resemblance to a purely militant, strictly centralised organisation led in all its minutest details by the single will of the organised Russian government—which is our immediate enemy in the political struggle.

But that is not the case. As we have already pointed out many times, the economic struggle is a trade struggle, and for that reason it requires that the workers be organised according to trade and not only according to their place of employment. And this organisation by trade becomes all the more imperatively necessary, the more rapidly our employers organise in all sorts of companies and syndicates. Our state of diffusion and our primitiveness hinders this work of organisation, and in order that this work may be carried out, we must have a single, All-Russian organisation of revolutionists capable of undertaking the leadership of the All-Russian trade unions. We have already described above the type of organisation that is desired for this purpose, and now we shall add just a few words about this in connection with the question of our press.

Hardly any one will doubt the necessity for every Social-Democratic newspaper having a special section devoted to the trade-union (economic) struggle. But the growth of the trade-union movement compels us to think about the trade-union press. It seems to us, however, that with rare exceptions, it is not much use thinking of trade-union newspapers in Russia at the present time: That would be a luxury, and in many places we cannot even obtain our daily bread. The form of trade-union press that would suit the conditions of our illegal works and that is already called for at the present time is the *Trade-Union Pamphlet*. In these pamphlets, *legal* * and illegal material should be collected and organised, on conditions of labour in a given trade, on the various conditions prevailing in the various parts of Russia, on the principal demands advanced by the workers in a given trade, about the defects of the laws in relation to that trade, of the outstanding cases of workers' economic struggle in this trade, about the rudiments, the present state and the requirements of their trade-union organisations, etc. Such pamphlets would, in the first place, relieve our Social-Democratic press of a mass of trade details that interest only the workers employed in the given trade; secondly, they would record the results of our experience in the trade-union struggle, would preserve the material collected—which is now literally lost in a mass of leaflets and fragmentary correspondence—and would generalise this material. Thirdly, they could serve as material for the guidance of agitators, because conditions of labour change relatively slowly, the principal demands of the workers in a given trade hardly ever change (see for example the demands advanced by the weavers in the Moscow district in 1885 and in the St. Petersburg district in 1896), and a compilation of these demands and needs might serve

* Legal material is particularly important in this connection, but we have lagged behind very much in our ability systematically to collect and utilise it. It would not be an exaggeration to say that legal material alone would provide sufficient material for a trade-union pamphlet, whereas illegal material alone would not be sufficient. In collecting illegal material from workers, on questions like those dealt with in the publications of *Rabochaya Mysl*, we waste a lot of the efforts of revolutionists (whose place in this work, could very easily be taken by legal workers), and yet we never obtain good material because a worker who knows only a single department of a large factory, who knows the economic results but not the general conditions and standards of his work, cannot acquire the knowledge that is possessed by the office staff of a factory, by inspectors, doctors, etc., and which is scattered in petty newspaper correspondence, and in special, industrial, medical, Zemstvo and other publications.

I very distinctly remember my "first experiment," which I am not going to repeat. I spent many weeks "examining" a workingman, who came to visit me, about the conditions prevailing in the enormous factory at which he was employed. True, after great effort, I managed to obtain material for a description (of just one single factory!), but at the end of each interview the workingman would wipe the sweat from his brow, and say to me smilingly: "I would rather work overtime than reply to your questions!"

The more energetically we carry on our revolutionary struggle, the more the government will be compelled to legalise a part of the "trade-union" work, and by that will relieve us of part of our burden.

for years as an excellent handbook for agitators on economic questions in backward localities, or among backward strata of the workers. Examples of successful strikes, information about the higher standard of life, of better conditions of labour, in one district, would encourage the workers in other districts to take up the fight again and again. Fourthly, having made a start in generalising the trade-union struggle, and having in this way strengthened the contacts between the Russian trade-union movement and Socialism, the Social-Democrats would at the same time see to it that our trade-union work did not occupy either too small or too large a share of our general Social-Democratic work. A local organisation, that is cut off from the organisations in other towns, finds it very difficult, and sometimes almost impossible, to maintain a correct sense of proportion (and the example of *Rabochaya Mysl* shows what a monstrous exaggeration is sometimes made in the direction of trade unionism). But an All-Russian organisation of revolutionists, that stands undeviatingly on the basis of Marxism, leads the whole of the political struggle and possesses a staff of professional agitators, will never find it difficult to determine the proper proportion.

V

THE "PLAN" FOR AN ALL-RUSSIAN POLITICAL NEWSPAPER

"THE most serious blunder *Iskra* made in this connection," writes B. Krichevsky [*Rabocheye Dyelo*, No. 10, p. 30], accusing us of betraying a tendency to "convert theory into a lifeless doctrine by isolating it from practice"—"was in promoting its 'plan' for general party organisation" [*i. e.*, the article entitled "Where to Begin"] and Martynov echoes this idea by declaring that *Iskra's* tendency to belittle the march of the drab, every-day struggle in comparison with the propaganda of brilliant and complete ideas . . . was crowned by the plan for the organisation of a party that it advances in an article in No. 4, entitled "Where to Begin?" [*ibid.*, p. 61]. Finally, L. Nadezhdin has recently joined in the chorus of indignation against the "plan" (the quotation marks were meant to express sarcasm). In a pamphlet we have just received written by him, entitled *The Eve of Revolution* (published by the Revolutionary Socialist group, *Svoboda*, whose acquaintance we have already made), he declares that: "To speak now of an organisation to be linked up with an All-Russian newspaper means to propagate armchair ideas and armchair work" [p. 126], that it is a manifestation of "literariness," etc.

It does not surprise us that our terrorist agrees with the champions of the "forward march of the drab, every-day struggle," because we have already traced the roots of this intimacy between them in the chapters on politics and organisation. But we must here draw attention to the fact that L. Nadezhdin is the only one who has conscientiously tried to understand the ideas expressed in an article he disagrees with, and has made an attempt to reply to it, whereas *Rabocheye Dyelo* has said nothing that is material to the subject, but has tried only to confuse the question by a whole series of inappropriate, demagogic sallies. Unpleasant though the task may be, we must spend a little time on cleaning this Augean stable.

A. WHO WAS OFFENDED BY THE ARTICLE "WHERE TO BEGIN"?

We shall quote a bouquet of the expletives and exclamations that *Rabocheye Dyelo* hurled at us. "A newspaper cannot create a **party** organisation; on the contrary, a party organisation must create a newspaper. . . ." "A newspaper, standing *above* the party, *outside of its control* and independent of it, thanks to its having its own staff of agents. . . ." "By what miracle has *Iskra* forgotten about the actual existence of the Social-Democratic organisations of the party to which it belongs? . . ." "Those who possess firm principles and a corresponding plan are the supreme regulators of the real struggle of the party and dictate to it their plan. . . ." "The plan drives our lives and virile organisations into the kingdom of shadows and desires to call into being a fantastic network of agents. . . ." "If *Iskra's* plans were carried out, every trace of the Russian Social-Democratic Labour Party, which is growing up in Russia, would be completely wiped out. . . ." "The propagandist organ becomes an uncontrolled autocratic legislator for the whole of the practical revolutionary struggle. . . ." "What should be the attitude of our party towards the propsal for its *complete* subordination to an autonomous editorial board?", etc., etc.

As the reader can see from the contents and tone of the above quotations, *Rabocheye Dyelo feels offended*. But it is offended, not for its own sake, but for the sake of the organisations and committees of our party which it alleges *Iskra* desires to drive into the kingdom of shadows, and the traces of which it desires to obliterate. Terrible, isn't it? But a curious thing should be noted. The article "Where to Begin" appeared in May, 1901. The articles in *Rabocheye Dyelo* appeared in September, 1901. Now we are in the middle of January, 1902. During these five months, *not a single committee and not a single organisation of the party* (neither before nor after September) protested against this monster which desires to drive them into the kingdom of shadows; and yet scores and hundreds of communications from all parts of Russia have appeared during this period in *Iskra,* and in numerous local and non-local publications. How is it that those whom it is desired to drive into the kingdom of shadows are not aware of it and have not felt offended about it, but a third party is offended over it?

This is to be explained by the fact that the committees and other organisations are engaged in real work and do not play at "democracy." The committees read the article "Where to Begin," saw that it was an attempt "to work out a certain plan of organisation *by which the setting up of this organisation could be approached from all sides,*" and as they knew very well that *not one* of these "sides" will dream of "setting to work to build it" until it is convinced of its necessity, and of the correctness of the architectural plan, they naturally felt no offence at the boldness of the people who in *Iskra* said: "In view of the urgency and importance of the question, we take it upon ourselves to submit to our comrades an outline of a plan which is developed in greater detail in a pamphlet that we are preparing for the press." Assuming people were actuated by motives of good-will, would they not understand that if the comrades *accepted* the plan submitted to them, they would carry it out, not because they are "subordinate" but because they were convinced of its necessity for our common cause, and that if they *did not accept it*, then the "outline" (a pretentious word, is it not?) would remain merely an outline? Is it not sheer demagogy to oppose the outline of a plan, not only by "picking it to pieces" and advising comrades to reject it, but also by *inciting* those inexperienced in revolutionary affairs against the authors of the plan *merely on the grounds* that they *dare* to "legislate" and come out as the "supreme regulators," *i. e.*, because they dare to *propose* an outline of a plan? Can our party develop and make progress if an attempt to *broaden* the outlook of local party workers so that they may be able to appreciate broader views, tasks, plans, etc., is objected to, not on the ground that these views are wrong, but on the grounds that the very "desire" to *broaden* is "offensive"? L. Nadezhdin also "picked our plan to pieces," but he did not sink to such demagogy—demagogy that cannot be explained by naïveté or by primitiveness of political views. Right from the outset, he emphatically rejected the charge that we intended to establish an "inspectorship over the party." That is why Nadezhdin's criticism of the plan deserves serious treatment, while *Rabocheye Dyelo* deserves only to be treated with contempt.

But contempt for a writer, who sinks to shouting about "autocracy" and "subordination," does not relieve us of the duty of disentangling the confusion that such people create in the minds of their readers, and here we can demonstrate to the world the nature of the catchwords like "broad democracy." We are accused of forgetting the committees, of desiring or attempting to drive them into the kingdom of shadows, etc. How can we reply to these charges when, owing to considerations of secrecy, we are *not in a position* to tell the reader *anything* about our real relationships with the committees? The people who broadcast slashing accusations which excite the people appear to be ahead of us because of their recklessness and their neglect of the duty of a revolutionist carefully to conceal from the eyes of the world the relationships and contacts he has, which he is establishing or trying to establish. Naturally, we absolutely refuse once for all to compete with such people on the field of "democracy."

As for the reader who is not enlightened on all party affairs, the only way in which we can fulfil our duty to him is to tell him, not about what is and what is *im Werden* * but about a particle of what has taken place and what it is permissible to tell him in view of its being an event of the past.

The Bund hints that we are "pretenders"; ** the League abroad accuses us of attempting to obliterate all traces of the party. Gentlemen, you will get complete satisfaction when we relate to the public *four facts* concerning the past.

First fact.*** The members of one of the Leagues of Struggle, who took a direct part in the formation of our party, and in sending a delegate to the party congress which established the party, came to an agreement with one of the members of the *Iskra* group about the foundation of a special workers' library in order to satisfy the needs of the whole of the movement. The attempt to publish a library failed, and the pamphlets written for it: *The Tasks of Russian Social-Democrats*, and *The New Factory Act*,**** by a roundabout way, and through the medium of third parties, found their way abroad, and were there published.

Second fact. The members of the Central Committee of the Bund came to one of the members of the *Iskra* group with the proposal to organise what the Bund then described as a "literary laboratory." In making the proposal, they stated that unless this was done, the movement would retrogress very much. The result of these negotiations was the appearance of the pamphlet, *The Cause of Labour in Russia*.*****

* What is in the process of becoming.—*Ed.*
** *Iskra*, No. 8. The reply of the Central Committee of the Bund to our article on the national question.
*** We deliberately refrain from relating these facts in the order in which they occurred.
**** See V. I. Lenin, *Collected Works*, Vol. II.—*Ed.*
***** The author of this pamphlet asks me to state that this pamphlet, like the one he wrote previously, was sent to the League on the assumption that the editors of its publications were the Emancipation of Labour group (owing to certain circumstances, he could not then—February, 1899—know about the change in the editorship). This pamphlet will be republished by the League at an early date.

Third fact. The Central Committee of the Bund, *via* a provincial town, came to one of the members of *Iskra* with the proposal that he accept the post of editor of the revived *Rabochaya Gazeta* and, of course, received his consent. This proposal was later modified. The comrade in question was invited to act as a contributor, in view of a new arrangement that had been made with the editorial board. To this also consent was, of course, given. Articles were sent (which we managed to preserve); "Our Programme" which was a direct protest against Bernsteinism, against the change of policy in legal literature and in *Rabochaya Mysl;* "Our Immediate Tasks" ("The publication of a party organ that shall appear regularly and have close contacts with all the local groups"; the drawbacks of the prevailing "primitive methods"); "Urgent questions" (an examination of the argument that it is necessary *first of all* to develop the activities of local groups before undertaking the publication of a central organ; an insistence on the paramount importance of a "revolutionary organisation," and on the necessity of "developing organisation, discipline, and the technique of secrecy to the highest stage of perfection").* The proposal to resume publication of *Rabochaya Gazeta* was not carried out, and the articles were not published.

Fourth fact. A member of the committee that organised the second regular congress of our party communicated to a member of the *Iskra* group the programme of the congress, and proposed that group for the office of editing the revived *Rabochaya Gazeta.* This preliminary step, as it were, was later sanctioned by the committee to which this member belonged, and by the Central Committee of the Bund; the *Iskra* group was notified of the place and time of the congress and (not being sure of being able, for certain reasons, to send a delegate to the congress), drew up a written report for the congress. In this report, the idea was suggested that the mere election of a central committee would not only not solve the question of the amalgamation at a time like this, when complete confusion reigns, but may even compromise the grand idea of establishing a party, in the event of an early and complete discovery of the organisation, and a raid by the police, which was more than likely in view of the prevailing lack of secrecy, and that therefore, a beginning should be made by inviting all committees and all other organisations to support the revived common organ, which will

* See V. I. Lenin, *Collected Works,* Vol. II.—*Ed.*

establish *real contacts* between all the committees and *really* train a group of leaders to lead the whole movement; that the committees and the party could very easily transform this group into a central committee as soon as the group had grown and become strong. The congress, however, never took place owing to a number of police raids and arrests; for reasons of secrecy, the report was destroyed, having been read only by several comrades including the representatives of one committee.

Let the reader now judge for himself the character of the methods employed by the Bund in hinting that we were pretenders, or by *Rabocheye Dyelo,* who accuses us of trying to relegate the committees to the kingdom of shadows, and to "substitute" an organisation for advocating the idea of a single newspaper for the organisation of a party. Yes, we did report to the committees, *on their repeated invitation,* on the necessity for accepting a definite plan of work in common. It was precisely for the party organisations that we drew up this plan, in articles published in *Rabochaya Gazeta,* and in the report to the party congress, again on the invitation of those who occupied such an influential position in the party that they took the initiative in its (actual) revival. And only after the *two-fold* attempt of the party organisation, *in conjunction with ourselves,* to revive the central organ of the party *officially* had failed, did we think it our bounden duty to publish an *unofficial* organ, in order that with this *third* attempt the comrades may have before them the results of an *experiment* and not merely problematical proposals. Now certain results of this experiment are available to the view of all, and all comrades may now judge as to whether we properly understood our duties, and what must be thought of people who strive to mislead those who are unacquainted with the immediate past, simply because they are chagrined at our having proved to some their inconsistency on the "national" question, and to others the inadmissibility of their waverings in matters of principle.

B. Can a Newspaper Be a Collective Organiser?

The main points in the article "Where to Begin" deal *precisely* with this question, and reply to it positively. As far as we know, the only attempt to examine this question and to reply to it in the negative, was made by L. Nadezhdin, whose argument we reproduce in full:

. . . The manner in which the question of the necessity for an All-Russian newspaper is presented in *Iskra*, No. 4, pleases us very much, but we cannot agree that such a presentation is suitable in an article bearing the title, "Where to Begin." Undoubtedly this is an extremely important matter, but neither a newspaper, nor a whole series of popular leaflets, nor a whole mountain of manifestoes, can serve as the basis for a militant organisation in revolutionary times. We must set to work to build up strong political organisations in the localities. We lack such organisations; we have been carrying on our work mainly among intelligent workers, while the masses have been engaged almost exclusively in the economic struggle. *If we do not build up strong political organisations locally, what will be the use of even an excellently organised all-Russian newspaper?* It will be a burning bush, burning without being consumed and consuming nothing! *Iskra* thinks that as a matter of fact people will gather around it, and they will organise. *But they will find it more interesting to gather and organise around something more concrete!* This something more concrete may be the extensive publication of local newspapers, the immediate setting to work to rally the forces of labour for demonstrations, constant work by local organisations among the unemployed (regularly distribute pamphlets and leaflets among them, convene meetings for them, call upon them to resist the government, etc.). We must organise live political work in the localities, and when the time comes to amalgamate on this real basis—it will not be an artificial, a paper amalgamation—it will not be by means of newspapers that such an amalgamation of local work into an All-Russian cause will be achieved! [*The Eve of the Revolution*, p. 54.]

We have emphasised the passages in this eloquent tirade which most strikingly illustrate the author's incorrect judgement of our plan, and the incorrectness of the point of view generally that he opposes to that of *Iskra*. Unless we set up strong political organisations in the localities—even an excellently organised All-Russian newspaper will be of no avail. Absolutely true. But the whole point is that *there is no other way of training* strong political organisations except through the medium of an All-Russian newspaper. The author missed the most important statement *Iskra* made *before it proceeded* to explain its "plan": That it was necessary "to call for the establishment of a revolutionary organisation, capable of combining all the forces, and of leading the movement *not only in name* but in deed, *i. e., that will be ready at any moment to support every protest and every outbreak*, and to utilise these for the purpose of increasing and strengthening the militant forces required for decisive battle." After the February and March events, every one will agree with this in principle, continues *Iskra*, but we do not need a solution of this problem in principle *but a practical solution of it*; we must immediately bring forward a definite plan of construction in order that every one may set to work to build *from every side*. And now we are again being dragged away from a practical solution towards something that is correct in principle, indisputable and great, but absolutely inadequate and absolutely incomprehensible to the broad masses of workers, namely, to "build up strong political organisations!" This is not the point that is now being discussed, most worthy author! The point is, *How* to train and what training it should be?

It is not true to say that "we have been carrying on our work mainly among intelligent workers, while the masses have been engaged almost exclusively in the economic struggle." Presented in such a form, this postulate goes wrong on the point which *Svoboda* always goes wrong on, and which is radically wrong, and that is, it sets up the intelligent workers in contrast to the "masses." Even the intelligent workers have been "engaged almost exclusively in the economic struggle" during the past few years. Moreover, the masses will never learn to conduct the political struggle until we help to *train* leaders for this struggle, both from among the intelligent workers and from among the intellectuals; and such leaders can be trained *solely* by systematic and every-day appreciation of *all* aspects of our political life, of *all attempts* at protest and struggle on the part of various classes and on various pretexts. Therefore, to talk about "training political organisations" and at the same time to *contrast* a "paper organisation" of a political newspaper to "live political work in the localities" is simply ridiculous! Why, *Iskra* has adapted its "plan" for a newspaper to the "plan" for creating a "militant preparedness" to support the unemployed movement, peasant revolts, discontent among the Zemstvoists, "popular indignation against the reckless tsarist Bashi-Buzuks," etc. Every one who is at all acquainted with the movement knows perfectly well that the majority of local organisations *never dream* of these things, that many of the prospects of "live political work" *have never* been realised by a single organisation, that the attempt to call attention to the growth of discontent and protest among the Zemstvo intelligentsia rouses feelings of consternation and amazement in Nadezhdin ("Good Lord, is this newspaper intended for the Zemstvoists?"— *The Eve of the Revolution*, p. 129), among the Economists (Letter to *Iskra* No. 12) and among many of the practical workers. Under these circumstances, it is possible to "begin" *only* by stirring up people *to think* about all these things, to stir them up to summarise and generalise all the flashes of discontent and active struggle. "Live political work" can be commenced in our time, when Social-Democratic tasks are being degraded, *exclusively* with live political education, which is impossible unless we have a frequently issued and properly distributed All-Russian newspaper.

Those who regard *Iskra's* "plan" as a manifestation of literariness have totally failed to understand the substance of the plan, and imagine that what is suggested as the most suitable means for the present time is the ultimate goal. These people have not taken the trouble to study the two comparisons that were drawn to illustrate the plan proposed. *Iskra* wrote: The publication of an All-Russian political newspaper must be *the main line* that must guide us in our work of unswervingly developing, deepening, and expanding this organisation (*i. e.*, a revolutionary organisation always prepared to support every protest and every outbreak). Pray tell me: When a bricklayer lays bricks in various parts of an enormous structure, the like of which has never been seen before, is it a "paper" line that he uses to help him to find the correct place to place each brick, to indicate to him the ultimate goal of the work as a whole, to enable him to use not only every brick but even every piece of brick, which, joining with the bricks placed before and after it, forms a complete and all-embracing line? And are we not now passing through a period in our party life, when we have bricks and bricklayers, but we lack the guiding line, visible to all, by which to guide our movements? Let them shout that in stretching out the line, we desire to command. Had we desired to command, gentlemen, we would have written on the title page, not *"Iskra,* No. 1,"* but *"Rabochaya Gazeta,* No. 3,"* as we were invited to do by a number of comrades, and *as we had a perfect right to do* after the events related above took place. But we did not do that. We wished to have our hands free to conduct an irreconcilable struggle against all pseudo-Social-Democrats; we wanted our line of policy, if properly laid, to be respected because it was correct, and not because it was carried out by an official organ.

"The question of combining local activity in central organs runs in a vicious circle," L. Nadezhdin tells us pedantically, "for this requires homogeneous elements, and this homogeneity can be created only by something that combines; but this combining element may be the product of strong local organisations which at the present time are not distinguished for their homogeneity." This

truism is as hoary and indisputable as the one that: We must build up strong political organisations. And is equally barren. *Every* question "runs in a vicious circle" because the whole of political life is an endless chain consisting of an infinite number of links. The whole art of politics lies in finding the link that can be least torn out of our hands, the one that is most important at the given moment, the one that guarantees the command of the whole chain, and having found it, to cling to that link as tightly as possible.*
If we possessed a staff of experienced bricklayers who had learned to work so well together that they could dispense with a guiding line and could place their bricks exactly where they are required without one (and speaking abstractly, this is by no means impossible), then perhaps we might seize upon some other link. But the unfortunate thing is that we have no experienced bricklayers trained to teamwork, that bricks are often laid where they are not needed at all, that they are not laid according to the general line, and are so scattered about that the enemy can shatter the structure as if it were made not of bricks but of sand.

Here is the other comparison:

A newspaper is not merely a collective propagandist and collective agitator, it is also a collective organiser. In that respect it *can be compared to the scaffolding* erected around a building in construction; it marks the contours of the structure, and facilitates communication between the builders, permitting them to distribute the work, and to view the common results achieved by their organised labour.**

Does this sound anything like the attempt of an armchair author to exaggerate his rôle? The scaffolding put up around a building is not required at all for habitation, it is made of the cheapest material, it is only put up temporarily and when finished with, as soon as the shell of the structure is completed, is destroyed. As for the building up of revolutionary organisations, experience shows that sometimes they may be built without scaffolding,—take the seventies

* Comrade Krichevsky and Comrade Martynov! I call your attention to this outrageous manifestation of "autocracy" "uncontrolled authority," "supreme regulating," etc. Just think of it: a desire to *possess* the whole chain!! Send in a complaint at once. Here you have a subject for two leading articles for No. 12 of *Rabocheye Dyelo!*
** Martynov, quoting the first sentence in this passage in *Rabocheye Dyelo* [No. 10, p. 62] left out the second sentence, as if desiring to emphasise by that either his unwillingness to discuss the essentials of the question, or his incapability of understanding it.

for example. But at the present time we cannot imagine that the building we require can be put up without scaffolding.

Nadezhdin disagrees with this, and says: "*Iskra* thinks that people will gather around it and will organise, *but they will find it more interesting to organise around something more concrete!*" So! so! "They will find it more interesting to gather around something more concrete. . . ." There is a Russian proverb which says: "Don't spit into the well, you may want to drink out of it." But there are people who do not object to drinking from a well which has been spat into. What despicable things our magnificent, legal "critics of Marxism" and illegal admirers of *Rabochaya Mysl* have said in the name of this—something more concrete! See how restricted our movement is by our own narrowness, lack of initiative, and hesitation and yet this is justified by the traditional argument about "finding it more interesting to gather around something more concrete!" And Nadezhdin, who regards himself as being particularly sensitive to "life," who so severely condemns "armchair" authors, who (with pretensions to being witty) charges *Iskra* with a weakness for seeing Economism everywhere, and who imagines that he stands far above this discrimination between the "orthodox" and the "critics,"—fails to see that with this sort of argument he is playing into the hands of the very narrowness with which he is so indignant and that he is drinking from a well that has actually been spat into! The sincerest indignation against narrowness, the most passionate desire to raise those who worship this narrowness from their knees, is insufficient if the indignant one is swept along without sail or rudder as "spontaneously" as the revolutionists of the seventies, if he clutches at such things as "excitative terror," "agrarian terror," "sounding-the-tocsin," etc. Glance at this something "more concrete" around which he thinks it is "much easier" to rally and organise: 1. Local newspapers; 2. Preparations for demonstrations; 3. Work among the unemployed. It will be seen at the very first glance that all these have been seized upon at random in order to be able to say something, for however we may regard them, it would be absurd to see in them anything especially adapted for the purpose of "rallying and organising." This very Nadezhdin a few pages further on says: "It is time we simply stated the fact that extremely petty work is being carried on in the localities, the committees are not doing a tenth of what they could do . . . the combining centres that we have at the present time are a pure fiction, they represent a sort of revolutionary bureaucracy, the members of which mutually appoint each other to the posts of generals; and so it will continue until strong local organisations grow up." These remarks while exaggerating the position somewhat, express many a bitter truth, but cannot Nadezhdin see the connection between the petty work carried on in the localities and the narrow outlook of the party workers, the narrow scope of their activities, which is inevitable in view of the lack of training of the party workers isolated in their local organisations? Has he, like the author of the article on organisation published in *Svoboda*, forgotten how the adoption of a broad local press (in 1898) was accompanied by a very strong intensification of Economism and "primitive methods"? Even if a broad local press could be established at all satisfactorily (and we have shown above that it is impossible save in very exceptional cases)—even then the local organs could not "rally and organise" *all* the revolutionary forces for a *general* attack upon the autocracy and for the leadership of a *united* struggle. Do not forget that we are here discussing *only* the "rallying," the organising significance of a newspaper, and we could put to Nadezhdin, who defends diffusiveness, the very question that he himself has already put ironically: "Has some one left us a legacy of 200,000 revolutionary organisers?" Furthermore, "preparations for demonstrations" cannot be set up in *contrast* to *Iskra's* plan for the one reason alone that this plan includes the organisation of the widest possible demonstrations *as one of its aims;* the point under discussion is the selection of the practical *means.* On this point also Nadezhdin has got confused and has lost sight of the fact that only already "rallied and organised" forces can "prepare for" demonstrations (which hitherto, in the overwhelming majority of cases, have taken place quite spontaneously) and we *lack precisely the ability* to rally and organise. "Work among the unemployed." Again the same confusion, for this too represents one of the military operations of mobilised forces and not a plan to mobilise the forces. The extent to which Nadezhdin underestimates the harm caused by our diffusion, by our lack of "200,000 men," can be seen from the following: Many (including Nadezhdin) have reproached *Iskra* with the paucity of the news it gives about unemployment and with the casual nature of the correspondence it publishes about the most common affairs of rural life. The reproach is justified, but *Iskra* is "guilty without sin." We strive to "draw a line" even through the countryside, but there are almost no bricklayers there, and we are *obliged* to encourage *every one* to send us information concerning even the most common facts in the hope that this will increase the number of our contributors in this field and will *train us all* at least to select the really most outstanding facts. But the material upon which we can train is so scanty that unless we collect it from all parts of Russia we will have very little to train upon at all. No doubt, one who possesses at least as much capacity as an agitator and as much knowledge of the life of the vagrant as apparently Nadezhdin has, could render priceless service to the movement by carrying on agitation among the unemployed—but such a one would be simply burying his talents if he failed to inform *all* Russian comrades of every step he took in his work, in order that others, who, in the mass, as yet lack the ability to undertake new kinds of work, may learn from his example.

Absolutely everybody now talks about the importance of unity, about the necessity for "rallying and organising," but the majority of us lack a definite idea of where to begin and how to bring about this unification. Every one will probably agree that if we "unite" say, the district circles in a given city, it will be necessary to have for this purpose *common institutions, i. e.,* not merely a common title of "League" but genuinely *common* work, exchange of material, experience, and forces, distribution of functions, not only in the given districts but in a whole city, according to special tasks. Every one will agree that a big secret apparatus will not pay its way (if one may employ a commercial expression) "with the resources" (in material and man power, of course) of a single district and that a single district will not provide sufficient scope for a specialist to develop his talents. But the same thing applies to the unification of a number of cities, because even such a field, like a single locality, *will prove,* and has already proved in the history of our Social-Democratic movement, to be too restricted: we have already dealt with this in detail above, in connection with political agitation and organisational work. We must first and foremost widen the field, establish *real* contacts between the cities, on the basis of *regular, common* work; for diffusion restricts the activities of our people who are "stuck in a hole" (to use the expression employed by a correspondent to *Iskra*), not knowing what is happening in the world; they have no one to learn from, do not know how to obtain or to satisfy their desire to engage in broad activities. And I continue to insist that we can *start* establishing *real* contacts only with the aid of a common newspaper, as a single, regular, All-Russian enterprise, which will summarise the results of all the diverse forms of activity and thereby *stimulate* our people to march forward untiringly along *all* the innumerable paths which lead to the revolution in the same way as all roads lead to Rome. If we do not want unity in name only, we must arrange for every local circle *immediately to assign*, say a fourth of its forces to *active* work for the *common* cause, and the newspaper will immediately convey to them * the general design, dimensions and character of this cause, will indicate to them precisely the most serious defects of All-Russian activity, where agitation is lacking and where contacts are weak, and point out which small wheel in the great general mechanism could be repaired or replaced by a better one. A circle that has not commenced to work yet, which is only just seeking work, could then start, not like a craftsman in a small separate workshop unaware of the development that has taken place in "industry," or of the general state of the given industry and the methods of production prevailing in it, but as a participant in an extensive enterprise that *reflects* the whole general revolutionary attack upon the autocracy. And the more perfect the finish of each little wheel will be, the larger the number of detail workers working for the common cause, the closer will our network become and the less consternation will inevitable police raids call forth in the common ranks.

The mere function of distributing a newspaper will help to establish *real* contacts (that is, if it were a newspaper worthy of the name, *i. e.*, if it is issued regularly, not once a month like a big magazine, but four times a month). At the present time, communication between cities on revolutionary business is an extreme rarity, and at all events an exception rather than the rule. If we had a newspaper, however, such communication would become the rule and would secure, not only the distribution of the newspaper, of course, but also (and what is more important) an interchange of

---

* A *reservation:* that is, if a given circle sympathises with the policy of that newspaper and considers it useful to become a collaborator, meaning by that, not merely a literary collaborator but a revolutionary collaborator generally. *Note for Rabocheye Dyelo:* among the revolutionists who attach value to the cause and not to playing at democracy, who do not separate "sympathy" from active and lively participation, this reservation is taken for granted.

experience, of material, of forces and of resources. The scope of organisational work would immediately become ever so much wider and the success of a single locality would serve as a standing encouragement to further perfection and a desire to utilise the experience gained by comrades working in other parts of the country. Local work would become far richer and more varied than it is now: political and economic exposures gathered from all over Russia would provide mental food to the workers of all trades and in *all stages of development,* would provide material and occasion for talks and readings on the most diverse subjects, which indeed will be suggested by hints in the legal press, by conversations among the public and by shamefaced government communications. Every outbreak, every demonstration, would be weighed and discussed from all its aspects all over Russia; it would stimulate a desire not to lag behind the rest, a desire to excel,—(we Socialists do not by any means reject all rivalry or all "competition!")—and consciously to prepare for that which at first appeared to spring up spontaneously, a desire to take advantage of the favourable conditions in a given district or at a given moment for modifying the plan of attack, etc. At the same time, this revival of local work would render superfluous that convulsive exertion of effort on the part of *all* local workers, working as if in the "throes of death" and the blunt invitation to join put to *every one* willing to perform some service, as is often done to-day when organising every single demonstration or publishing every single number of a local newspaper. In the first place the police would find it much more difficult to dig down to the "roots" because they would not know in what district to seek for them. Secondly, regular common work would train our people to regulate the force of a *given* attack in accordance with the strength of the forces of the given local detachment of the army (at the present time no one ever thinks of doing that because in nine cases out of ten these attacks occur spontaneously), and would facilitate the "transport" from one place to another, not only of literature, but also of revolutionary forces.

In the overwhelming majority of cases, these forces at the present time shed their blood in the cause of restricted local work, but under the circumstances we are discussing, occasions would constantly arise for transferring a capable agitator or organiser from one end of the country to the other. Beginning with short journeys on party business at the party's expense, our people would become accustomed to live at the expense of the party, would become professional revolutionists and would train themselves to become real political leaders.

And if indeed we succeeded in reaching a point when all, or at least a considerable majority of the local committees, local groups and circles actively took up work for the common cause we could, in the not distant future, establish a daily newspaper that would be regularly distributed in tens of thousands of copies over the whole of Russia. This newspaper would become a part of an enormous pair of smith's bellows that would blow every spark of class struggle and popular indignation into a general conflagration. Around what is in itself very innocent and very small, but in the full sense of the word a regular and *common* cause, an army of tried warriors would systematically gather and receive their training. On the ladders and scaffolding of this general organisational structure there would soon ascend Social-Democratic Zhelyabovs from among our revolutionists and Russian Bebels from among our workers who would take their places at the head of the mobilised army and rouse the whole people to settle accounts with the shame and the curse of Russia. That is what we ought to be dreaming about!

"We ought to dream!" I wrote these words and then got scared. It seemed to me that I was sitting at a "unity congress" and that opposite me were the editors and contributors of *Rabocheye Dyelo*. Comrade Martynov rises and turning to me says threateningly: "Permit me to enquire, has an autonomous editorial board the right to dream without first obtaining permission of the party committee?" He is followed by Comrade Krichevsky who (philosophically deepening the words of Comrade Martynov who had long ago deepened the words of Comrade Plekhanov) continues in the same strain even more threateningly: "I go further. I ask, has a Marxist any right at all to dream, knowing that according to Marx, man always sets himself achievable tasks and that tactics is a process of growth of tasks, which grow together with the party?"

The very thought of these menacing questions sends a cold shiver down my back and makes me wish for nothing except a place to conceal myself in. I will try to conceal myself behind the back of Pisarev.

"There are differences and differences," wrote Pisarev concerning the question of the difference between dreams and reality. "My dream may run ahead of the natural progress of events or may fly off at a tangent in a direction to which no natural progress of events will ever proceed. In the first case the dream will not cause any harm; it may even support and strengthen the efforts of toiling humanity. There is nothing in such dreams that would distort or paralyse labour power. On the contrary, if man were completely deprived of the ability to dream in this way, if he could never run ahead and mentally conceive in an entire and completed picture the results of the work he is only just commencing, then I cannot imagine what stimulus there would be to induce man to undertake and complete extensive and fatiguing work in the sphere of art, science and practical work. . . . Divergence between dreams and reality causes no harm if only the person dreaming believes seriously in his dream, if he attentively observes life, compares his observations with the airy castles he builds and if, generally speaking, he works conscientiously for the achievement of his fantasies. If there is some connection between dreams and life then all is well.

Now of this kind of dreaming there is unfortunately too little in our movement. And those most responsible for this are the ones who boast of their sober views, their "closeness" to the "concrete," *i. e.*, the representatives of legal criticism and of illegal "khvostism."

C. What Type of Organisation Do We Require?

From what has been said the reader will understand that our "tactics plan" consists in rejecting an immediate *call* for the attack, in demanding "a regular siege of the enemy fortress," or in other words, in demanding that all efforts be directed towards rallying, organising and *mobilising* permanent troops. When we ridiculed *Rabocheye Dyelo* for its leap from Economism to shouting for an attack (in *Listok Rabochevo Dyela*, No. 6, April, 1901) it of course hurled accusations against us of being "doctrinaire," of failing to understand our revolutionary duty, of calling for caution, etc. Of course we were not surprised to hear these accusations coming from those who totally lack balance and who evade all arguments by references to a profound "tactics-process," any more than we were surprised by the fact that these accusations were repeated by Nadezhdin who has a supreme contempt for durable programmes and tactical bases.

It is said that history never repeats itself. But Nadezhdin is exerting every effort to cause it to repeat itself and zealously imitates Tkachev in strongly condemning "revolutionary culturism," in shouting about "sounding the tocsin" about a special "eve of the revolution point-of-view," etc. Apparently, he has forgotten the well-known epigram which says: If an original historical event represents a tragedy, the copy of it is only a farce. The attempt to seize power, after the ground for the attempt had been prepared by the preaching of Tkachev and carried out by means of the "terrifying" terror which did really terrify was majestic, but the "excitative" terror of a little Tkachev is simply ridiculous and is particularly ridiculous when it is supplemented by the idea of an organisation of average workers.

"If *Iskra* would only emerge from its sphere of literariness," wrote Nadezhdin, "it would realise that these [the working man's letter to *Iskra* No. 7, etc.] are symptoms of the fact that soon, very soon the 'attack' will commence, and to talk now [*sic!*] about organisations linked up with an All-Russian newspaper is simply to give utterance to armchair thoughts and to do armchair work." What unimaginable confusion this is: on the one hand excitative terror and an "organisation of average workers" accompanied by the opinion that it is "much easier" to gather around something "more concrete" like a local newspaper,—and on the other hand, to talk "now" about an All-Russian organisation means to give utterance to armchair thoughts, or, to speak more frankly and simply, "Now" is already too late! But what about "the extensive organisation of local newspapers,"—is it not too late for that my dear L. Nadezhdin? And compare this with *Iskra's* point-of-view and tactics: excitative terror—is nonsense; to talk about an organisation of average workers and about the *extensive* organisation of local newspapers means to open the door wide for Economism. We must speak about a single All-Russian organisation of revolutionists and it will never be too late to talk about that until the real, and not the paper attack, commences.

Yes, as far as our situation in regard to organisation is concerned, it is far from brilliant, continues Nadezhin. Yes, *Iskra* is absolutely right when it says that the mass of our military forces consist of volunteers and insurgents. . . . You do very well in thus soberly presenting the state of our forces. But why in doing so do you forget that *the crowd is not ours* and, consequently, *it will not ask us* when to commence military operations, it will simply go and "rebel." . . . When the crowd itself breaks out with its elemental destructive force it *may* overwhelm and crush the "regular troops" to which all may have rallied but which had *not managed* in time to establish itself as an extremely systematic organisation. [Our italics.]

Astonishing logic! *Precisely because* the "crowd is not ours," it is stupid and reprehensible to call for an "attack" this very minute, because an attack must be made by permanent troops and not by a spontaneous outburst of the crowd. It is precisely because the crowd *may* overwhelm and crush permanent troops that we must without fail "manage" to keep up with the spontaneous rise of the masses in our work of "establishing an extremely systematic organisation" among the permanent troops, for the more we "manage" to establish such an organisation the more probable will it be that the permanent troops will not be overwhelmed by the crowd, but will take their place at the head of the crowd. Nadezhdin drops into confusion because he imagines that these systematically organised troops are engaged in something that isolates them from the crowd, when as a matter of fact they are engaged exclusively in all-sided and all-embracing political agitation, *i. e.*, precisely in work that *brings them into closer proximity and merges* the elemental destructive force of the crowd with the conscious destructive force of the organisation of revolutionists. You gentlemen merely wish to throw the blame for your sins on the shoulders of others. For it is precisely the *Svoboda* group that includes terror in its *programme* and by that calls for an organisation of terrorists, and such an organisation would really prevent our troops from coming into proximity with the crowd which, unfortunately, is still not ours, and which unfortunately, does not yet ask us, or rarely asks us when and how to commence military operations.

"We will overlook the revolution itself," continues Nadezhdin in his effort to scare *Iskra*, "in the same way as we overlooked recent events which hurled themselves upon us like a bolt from the blue." This sentence together with the one quoted above clearly demonstrates the absurdity of the "eve of the revolution point-of-view" invented by *Svoboda*.* To speak frankly, this special point-of-view" amounts to this that it is too late "now" to discuss and prepare. If that is the case, oh most worthy opponent of "literariness," what was the use of writing a pamphlet of 132 pages on "Questions of Theory and Tactics"? ** Don't you think that it

* "The Eve of the Revolution," p. 62.
** In his *Review of Questions of Theory*, L. Nadezhdin made almost no contribution whatever to the discussion of questions of theory apart perhaps from the following passage which appears to be a very peculiar one from the "eve of the revolution point-of-view": "Bernsteinism, on the whole, is losing its acuteness for us at the present moment, as also is the question as to whether Mr. Adamovich has proved that Mr. Struve has already deserved dismissal or on the contrary whether Mr. Struve will refute Mr. Adamovich and will refuse to resign—it really makes no difference, because the hour of the revolution has struck" [p. 110]. One can hardly imagine a more striking

would have been more becoming for the "eve of the revolution point-of-view" to have issued 132,000 leaflets containing the brief appeal: "Kill them!"?

Those who place national political agitation as the cornerstone of their programme, *their tactics and their organisational work* as *Iskra* does, stand the least risk of overlooking the revolution. The people who were engaged over the whole of Russia in weaving a network of organisations to be linked up with an All-Russian news-paper not only did not overlook the spring events, but on the contrary, they enabled us to foretell them. Nor did they overlook the demonstrations that were described in *Iskra*, Nos. 13 and 14: on the contrary, they took part in those demonstrations, clearly appreciating their duty to come to the aid of the spontaneously rising crowd and while rendering aid, at the same time, through the medium of the newspaper, to make closer acquaintance with these demonstrations and to place their experience at the disposal of all Russian comrades. And if they live they will not overlook the revolution which first and foremost will demand of us experience in agitation, ability to support (in a Social-Democratic manner) every protest and ability to direct the spontaneous movements, and to guard them from the mistakes of friends and the traps of enemies!

This brings us to the final argument that compels us to insist particularly upon a plan of organisation that shall be centred around an All-Russian newspaper to be brought about by means of joint work for the establishment of a common newspaper. Only such an organisation will secure *flexibility* necessary for the Social-Democratic militant organisation, *i. e.*, an ability to adapt itself immediately to the most diverse and rapidly changing conditions of struggle, an ability to "renounce an open fight against overwhelming and concentrated forces, and yet capable of taking advantage of the awkwardness and immobility of the enemy and attack at a time and place where he least expects attack." *   It would be a

illustration of L. Nadezhdin's infinite disregard for theory. We have proclaimed "the eve of the revolution"—*therefore* "it really makes no difference" whether the orthodox Marxists will succeed in driving the critics from their positions or not!! And our wiseacre fails to see that it is precisely in the time of revolution that we stand in need of the results of our theoretical combats with the critics in order to be able resolutely to combat their *practical* positions!

* *Iskra*, No. 4, "Where to Begin." "Revolutionary culturists who do not accept the eve of the revolution point-of-view, are not in the least disturbed by the prospect of working for a long period of time," writes Nadezhdin

grievous error indeed to build up the party organisation in the expectation only of outbreaks and street fighting, or only upon the "forward march of the drab, every-day struggle." We must *always* carry on our every-day work and always be prepared for everything, because very frequently, it is almost impossible to foresee beforehand when periods of outbreaks will give way to periods of calm. And even in those cases when it is possible to do so, it will not be possible to utilise this foresight for the purpose of reconstructing our organisation, because in an autocratic country these changes from turmoil to calm take place with astonishing rapidity and are sometimes due merely to a single night raid by the tsarist janizaries. And the revolution itself must not by any means be regarded as a single act (as Nadezhdin apparently imagines) but as a series of more or less powerful outbreaks rapidly alternating with more or less intense calm. For that reason, the principal content of the activity of our party organisation, the "trick" of this activity should be, to carry on work that is possible and necessary both in the period of the most powerful outbreaks as well as in periods of complete calm, that is to say: work of political agitation linked up over the whole of Russia, that will enlighten all aspects of life and will be carried on among the broadest possible strata of the masses. But this work *cannot possibly be carried on* in contemporary Russia without an All-Russian newspaper, issued very frequently. An organisation that is built up around this newspaper, an organisation of *collaborators* of this paper (collaborators in the broad sense of the word, *i. e.*, all those working for it) will be ready *for everything*, from protecting the honour, the prestige, and continuity of the party in periods of acute revolutionary "depression" to preparing for, commencing and carrying out the *national armed insurrection.*

Indeed, picture to yourselves a very ordinary occurrence with us,

[p. 62]. On this we shall observe: unless we are able to devise political tactics and an organisational plan based precisely upon calculations for *work over a long period of time* and at the same time, *in the very process of this work,* put our party into readiness to spring to its post and fulfil its duty at the very first, even unexpected, call, as soon as the progress of events becomes accelerated, we will prove to be but miserable political adventurers. Only Nadezhdin, who only yesterday began to describe himself as a Social-Democrat, can forget that the aim of Social-Democracy is radically to transform the conditions of life of the whole of humanity and that for that reason it is not permissible for Social-Democrats to be "disturbed" by the question of the duration of the work.

—the complete discovery and arrest of our organisation in one or several localities. In view of the fact that *all* the local organisations lack *a single*, common regular task, such raids frequently result in the interruption of our work for many months. If, however, all the local organisations had one common task, then, in the event of a serious raid, two or three energetic persons could in the course of a few weeks establish new youth circles, which, as is well known, spring up very quickly even now, and link them up with the centre, and when this common task, which has been interrupted by the raid, is apparent to all, the new circles could spring up and link themselves up with it even more rapidly.

On the other hand, picture to yourselves a popular uprising. Probably every one will now agree that we must think of this uprising and prepare for it. But *how* to prepare for it? Surely the Central Committee cannot appoint agents to go to all the districts for the purpose of preparing for the uprising! Even if we had a Central Committee it could achieve nothing by making such appointments considering the conditions prevailing in contemporary Russia. On the contrary, a network of agents * that would automatically be created in the course of establishing and distributing a common newspaper would not have to "sit around and wait" for the call to rebellion, but would carry on the regular work that would guarantee the highest probability of success in the event of a rebellion. Such work would strengthen our contacts with the broadest strata of the masses of the workers and with all those strata who are discontented with the autocracy and who are so important to have in the event of an uprising. It is precisely such work that would help to cultivate the ability properly to estimate the general political situation and consequently, the ability to select the proper moment for the uprising. It is precisely such work that would train *all* local organisations to respond simultaneously to the same political

* Alas, alas! Again I have let slip that awful word "agents" which jars so awfully on the democratic ear of Martynov! I wonder why this word did not offend the sensibilities of the heroes of the seventies and yet offends the amateurs of the nineties? I like the word, bcause it clearly and distinctly indicates the *common cause* to which all the agents bend their thoughts and actions and if I had to replace this word by another, the only word I would select would be the word "collaborator" if it did not suggest literariness and diffusiveness. The thing we need is a militant organism of agents. The numerous (particularly abroad) Martynovs whose favourite pastime is "playing at generals" may instead of saying "passport agent" prefer to say, "Chief of the Special Department for Supplying Revolutionists with Passports," etc.

questions, incidents and events that excite the whole of Russia, to react to these "events" in the most vigorous, uniform and expedient manner possible; for is not rebellion in essence the most vigorous, most uniform and most expedient "reaction" of the whole people to the conduct of the government? And finally, such work would train all revolutionary organisations all over Russia to maintain the most continuous and at the same time the most secret contact with each other, which will create *real* Party unity,—for without such contacts it will be impossible collectively to discuss the plan of rebellion and to take the necessary preparatory measures on the eve of it, which must be kept in the strictest secrecy.

In a word, the "plan for an All-Russian political newspaper" does not represent the fruits of the work of armchair workers, infected with dogmatism and literariness (as it seemed to those who failed to study it properly), on the contrary it is a practical plan to commence immediately to prepare on all sides for the uprising, while at the same time never for a moment forgetting the ordinary, every-day work.

CONCLUSION

THE history of Russian Social-Democracy can be divided into three distinct periods:

The first period covers about ten years, approximately the years 1884 to 1894. This was the period when the theory and the programme of Social-Democracy germinated and took root. The number of adherents to the new tendency in Russia could be counted in units. Social-Democracy existed without a labour movement; it was, as it were, in its period of gestation.

The second period covers three or four years—1894-1898. In this period Social-Democracy appeared in the world as a social movement, as the rising of the masses of the people, as a political party. This is the period of its infancy and adolescence. Social-Democratic ideas spread among the intelligentsia like an epidemic and they became entirely absorbed in the fight against Populism, in going among the workers, and the latter, in their turn, were entirely absorbed in fomenting strikes. The movement made enormous strides. The majority of the leaders were very young people who had by no means reached the "age of thirty-five," which to N. Mikhailovsky appears to be a sort of natural borderline. Owing to their youth, they proved to be untrained for practical work and they left the scene with astonishing rapidity. But in the majority of cases the scope of their work was extremely wide. Many of them began their revolutionary thinking as Narodovolists. Nearly all of them in their early youth enthusiastically worshipped the terrorist heroes. It was a great wrench to abandon the captivating impressions of these heroic traditions and it was accompanied by the breaking off of personal relationships with people who were determined to remain loyal to *Narodnaya Volya* and for whom the young Social-Democrats had profound respect. The struggle compelled them to educate themselves, to read the illegal literature of all tendencies and to study closely the questions of legal Populism. Trained in this struggle, Social-Democrats went into the labour movement without "for a moment" forgetting the theories of Marxism which illumined their path or the task of overthrowing the autocracy. The formation of the party in the spring of 1898 was the most striking and at the same time the *last* act of the Social-Democrats in this period.

The third period, as we have seen, began in 1897 and definitely replaced the second period in 1898 (1898—?). This was the period of confusion, disintegration, and vacillation. In the period of adolescence the youth's voice breaks. The voice of Russian Social-Democracy in this period began to break, began to strike a false note—on the one hand, in the productions of Messrs. Struve and Prokopovich, Bulgakov and Berdyaev, on the other hand in the productions of V. I-na and R. M., B. Krichevsky and Martynov. But it was only the leaders who wandered from the path; the movement itself continued to grow and advanced by enormous strides. The proletarian struggle spread to new strata of the workers over the whole of Russia and at the same time indirectly stimulated the revival of the democratic spirit among the students and among other strata of the population. The consciousness of the leaders, however, shrank before the breadth and power of the spontaneous rising; among Social-Democrats, a different streak predominated—a streak of party workers who had been trained almost exclusively on "legal" Marxian literature, and the more the spontaneity of the masses called for consciousness, the more they lacked consciousness. The leaders not only lagged behind in regard to theory ("freedom of criticism") and practice ("primitiveness") but even tried to justify their backwardness by all sorts of high-flown arguments. Social-Democracy was degraded to the level of trade unionism in legal literature by the Brentanoists and in illegal literature by the Khvostists. The programme of the *Credo* began to be put into operation, especially when the "primitiveness" of the Social-Democrats caused a revival of non-Social-Democratic revolutionary tendencies.

And if the reader reproaches me for having dealt in excessive detail with *Rabocheye Dyelo*, I will say to him in reply: *Rabocheye Dyelo* acquired "historical" significance because it most strikingly reflected the "spirit" of this third period.* It was not the consistent R. M. but the weathercock Krichevskys and Martynovs who could properly express the confusion and vacillation, and the readiness to

---

* I could also reply in the German proverb: *Den Sack schägt man, den Esel meint man.* It was not *Rabocheye Dyelo* alone that was carried away by the fashion of "criticism" but also *the masses of practical workers and theoreticians;* they became confused over the question of spontaneity and slipped from the Social-Democratic to the trade-union conception of our political and organisational tasks.

make concessions to "criticism," to Economism and to terrorism. It is not the lofty contempt for practical work displayed by the worshippers of the "absolute" that is characteristic of this period, but the combination of pettifogging practice and utter disregard for theory. It was not so much the downright rejection of "grand phrases" that the heroes of this period engaged in as in their vulgarisation: Scientific Socialism ceased to be a complete revolutionary theory and became a petty-bourgeois idea "freely" diluted with the contents of every new German textbook that appeared; the slogan "class struggle" did not impel them forward to wider and more strenuous activity but served as a soothing syrup, because (*sic!*) the "economic struggle is inseparably linked up with the political struggle"; the idea of a party did not serve as a call for the creation of a militant organisation of revolutionists, but was used to justify some sort of a "revolutionary bureaucracy" and infantile playing at "democracy."

When this third period will come to an end and the fourth period will commence, we do not know (at all events it is already heralded by many symptoms). Just now we are passing from the sphere of history into the sphere of the present and partly into the sphere of the future. But we firmly believe that the fourth period will see the consolidation of militant Marxism, that Russian Social-Democracy will emerge from the crisis in the full strength of manhood, that a "new guard" will arise, that instead of the present rear-guard of opportunists, we will have a genuine vanguard of the most revolutionary class.

In the sense of calling for such a "new guard" and summing up as it were all that has been expounded above, my reply to the question: "What is to be done?" can be put briefly: Liquidate the Third Period.

APPENDIX

THE ATTEMPT TO UNITE *ISKRA* WITH *RABOCHEYE DYELO*

I⊤ remains for us to describe the organisational tactics *Iskra* adopted towards *Rabocheye Dyelo*. These tactics have been already fully expressed in *Iskra*, No. 1, in an article entitled "The Split in the League of Russian Social-Democrats Abroad." * From the outset we adopted the point-of-view that the *real* League of Russian Social-Democrats Abroad, which at the first congress of our party was recognised as the party's representative abroad, had *split* into two organisations;—that the question of the party's representation remains an open one and that the settlement reached at the International Congress at Paris by the election of two members to represent Russia on the International Socialist Bureau, one from each of the two sections of the divided League, was only a temporary and conditional settlement. We declared that on essentials *Rabocheye Dyelo was wrong;* in principie we emphatically took the side of the Emancipation of Labour group, but at the same time we refused to enter into the details of the split and noted the services rendered by the League in the sphere of purely practical work.**

Consequently, ours was, to a certain extent, a waiting policy; we made a concession tc the opinion prevailing among the majority of the Russian Social-Democrats that the most determined opponents of Economism could work hand in hand with the "League" because, it was said, the "League" has frequently declared its agreement in principle with the Emancipation of Labour group and that it did not claim an independent position on fundamental questions of theory and tactics. The correctness of the position we took up has been proved indirectly by the fact that almost simultaneously with the publication of the first number of *Iskra* [December, 1900] three members separated from the League and formed the so-called "Group of Initiators" and offered their services: 1. To the foreign section of the *Iskra* organisation; 2. To the Revolutionary Social-

* See article of the same title, *The Iskra Period*, Book I, p. 65.—*Ed.*
** Our opinion of the split was based not only upon a perusal of the literature on the subject but also on information gathered by several members of our organisation who had been abroad.

Democrat Organisation; and 3. To the "League" as mediators in negotiations for reconciliation. It is true that when a speaker related these facts at the "Unity" Congress last year, a member of the Management Committee of the "League" declared that their rejection of the offer was due entirely to the fact that the League was dissatisfied with the composition of the Initiators' group. While I consider it my duty to quote this explanation I cannot, however, refrain from observing that the explanation is an unsatisfactory one; knowing that two organisations had agreed to enter into negotiations, the "League" could have approached them through other intermediaries, or directly.

In the spring of 1901 both *Zarya* [No. 1, April] and *Iskra* [No. 4, May] entered into open polemics with *Rabocheye Dyelo*. *Iskra* particularly attacked the "historical turn" taken by *Rabocheye Dyelo* which, in its *April* supplement, and consequently after the spring events, revealed instability in regard to terror, and the calls for "blood," with which many had been carried away at the time. Notwithstanding these polemics, the "League" agreed to the resumption of negotiations for reconciliation through the mediation of a new group of "conciliators." A preliminary conference of representatives of the three organisations named above took place in June at which a draft agreement was drawn up on the basis of a detailed "agreement on principles" that was published by the "League" in the pamphlet *Two Congresses* and by the League in the pamphlet entitled *Documents of the Unity Congress.**

The contents of this agreement on principles (or as it is more frequently named, the Resolutions of the June Conference), clearly shows that we put forward as an absolute condition for unity *the most emphatic* repudiation of all manifestations of opportunism generally and of Russian opportunism in particular. Paragraph 1 reads: "We repudiate every attempt to introduce opportunism into the proletarian class struggle—attempts which are expressed in so-called Economism, Bernsteinism, Millerandism, etc." "The sphere of Social-Democratic activities include . . . intellectual struggle against all opponents of revolutionary Marxism" [4, C]; "In every

* The "League," in quotation marks, is the section of the League of Russian Social-Democrats Abroad that supported *Rabocheye Dyelo*, and the League, without quotation marks, is that section which supported *Iskra*. In the Russian text the former is described as the "Soyus," which means League, and the latter as "Liga," and in this way the two sections were distinguished from one another.—*Ed.*

sphere of organisational and agitational activity Social-Democracy must not for a moment forget that the immediate task of the Russian proletariat is—to overthrow the autocracy" [5, A]; ". . . agitation, not only on the basis of the every-day struggle between wage labour and capital" [5, B]; ". . . not recognising . . . stages of purely economic struggles and of struggles for partial political demands" [5, C]; ". . . we consider important for the movement criticism of the tendency which elevates primitiveness . . . and restrictedness of the lower forms of the movement into a principle" [5, C-D]. Even a complete outsider, who has read these resolutions at all attentively, will have realised from the very way in which they are formulated that they are directed against those who are opportunists and Economists, against those who, even for a moment, forget about the task of overthrowing the autocracy, who recognise the theory of stages, who have elevated narrowness to a principle, etc. And any one who has any acquaintance at all with the polemics conducted by the Emancipation of Labour group, *Zarya* and *Iskra* against *Rabocheye Dyelo*, cannot but be convinced that these resolutions repudiate point by point the very errors into which *Rabocheye Dyelo* had wandered. Consequently, when one of the members of the "League" declared at the "Unity" Congress that the articles in No. 10 of *Rabocheye Dyelo* were prompted, not by a new "historical turn" on the part of the "League," but by the fact that the resolutions were too "abstract," * this assertion was quite justly ridiculed by one of the speakers. The resolutions are not abstract in the least, he said, they are incredibly concrete: a single glance at them is sufficient to see that there is a "catch" in this.

The latter remark served as the occasion for a characteristic episode at the congress. On the one hand, B. Krichevsky seized upon the word "catch" in the belief that this was a slip of the tongue which betrayed our evil intentions ("To set a trap") and pathetically exclaimed: "A catch, for whom?" "Yes, indeed, for whom?"— Plekhanov rejoined sarcastically. "I will stimulate Comrade Plekhanov's perspicacity," replied B. Krichevsky, "I will explain to him that the trap was set *for the editorial board of Rabocheye Dyelo* (general laughter), "but we have not allowed ourselves to be caught!" (A remark from the left: all the worse for you!) On the other hand, a member of the Borba group (the conciliators), in opposing the "League's" amendment to the resolution and wishing

* This expression is repeated in *Two Congresses*, p. 25.

to defend our speaker, declared that obviously the word "catch" was dropped in the heat of polemics.

For my part, I think the speaker responsible for uttering the word under discussion was not at all pleased with this "defence." I think the word "catch" was a "true word spoken in jest": We have always accused *Rabocheye Dyelo* of instability and vacillation and, naturally, we *had* to try to *catch* it in order to put a stop to this vacillation. There is not the slightest suggestion of evil intent in this, for we were discussing instability of principles. And we succeeded in "catching" the "League" in such a comradely manner * that B. Krichevsky himself and one other member of the Managing Committee of the "League" signed the June resolutions.

The articles in *Rabocheye Dyelo*, No. 10 (our comrades saw this number for the first time when they arrived at the congress, a few days before the meetings started), clearly showed that the "League" had taken a new turn in the period between the summer and the autumn: the Economists had again got the upper hand on the editorial board, which turned with every "wind," and the board again defended "the most pronounced Bernsteinists," "freedom of criticism" and "spontaneity," and through the mouth of Martynov began to preach the "theory of restricting" the sphere of our political influence (for the alleged purpose of making this influence more complex). Once again Parvus' apt observation that it was difficult to catch an opportunist with a formula was proved correct. An opportunist will put his name to *any* formula and as readily abandon it, because opportunism is precisely a lack of definite and firm principles. To-day, the opportunists have repudiated *all* attempts to introduce opportunism, repudiated *all* narrowness, solemnly promised "never for a moment to forget about the task of overthrowing the autocracy," to carry on "agitation not only on the

* Precisely: In the introduction to the June resolutions we said that Russian Social-Democracy as a whole always took its stand on the basis of the principles of the Emancipation of Labour group and that the "League's" merit lay particularly in its publishing and organising activity. In other words, we expressed our complete readiness to forget the past and to recognise the usefulness (for the cause) of the work of our comrades of the "League" *on the condition* that it completely ceased the vacillation which we tried to "catch." Any impartial person reading the June resolutions will so interpret them. If, now the "League" after having *caused* a split by its new turn towards Economism (in its articles in No. 10 and in the amendments), solemnly accuses us of *prevaricating* [*Two Congresses*, p. 30] because of what we said about its merits, then, of course, such an accusation can only raise a smile.

basis of the every-day struggle between wage labour and capital," etc., etc. But to-morrow they will change their form of expression and revert to their old tricks on the pretext of defending spontaneity and the forward march of the drab every-day struggle, of proclaiming demands promising palpable results, etc. By asserting that in the articles in No. 10 "the 'League' did not and does not now see any heretical departure from the general principles of the draft adopted at the conference" [*Two Congresses*, p. 26], the "League" reveals a complete lack of ability, or a lack of desire, to understand the essential points of the disagreements.

After the appearance of *Rabocheye Dyelo*, No. 10, only one thing remained for us to do and that was to open a general discussion in order to ascertain whether all the members of the "League" agree with these articles and with its editorial board. The "League" is particularly displeased with us because of this and accuses us of sowing discord in the "League," of not minding our own business, etc. These accusations are obviously unfounded because with an elected board which "turns" with every breeze, everything depends precisely upon the direction of the wind, and we defined the direction of the wind at private meetings at which no one, except members of the organisations who had gathered together for the purpose of uniting, were present. The amendments to the June resolutions submitted in the name of the "League" have removed the last shadow of a hope of an agreement. The amendments are documentary evidence of the new turn towards Economism and of the fact that the majority of the members of the "League" are in agreement with *Rabocheye Dyelo*, No. 10. Amendments were moved to delete the words "so-called Economism" from the reference in the resolution to manifestations of opportunism (on the pretext that "the sense" of these three words "was vague"—but if that were so, all that was required was a more precise definition of the nature of a widespread error), and to delete "Millerandism" (although B. Krichevsky defended it in *Rabocheye Dyelo*, Nos. 2 and 3, pp. 83-84, and still more openly in the *Vorwärts*).* Notwithstanding the fact that the June resolutions definitely indicated the tasks of Social-Democracy, *viz.*, "to guide *every* manifestation of the proletarian struggle against *all* forms of political, *economic* and social oppres-

---

* A controversy over this subject had started in the *Vorwärts* between its present editor, Kautsky, and the editorial board of *Zarya*. We shall not fail to acquaint the reader with the nature of this controversy.

sion," and by that called for the introduction of system and unity in all these manifestations of the struggle, the "League" added the absolutely superfluous sentence to the effect that "the economic struggle is a powerful stimulus to the mass movement" (taken by itself, this assertion cannot be disputed, but in view of the existence of narrow Economism it cannot but give occasion for false interpretations). More than that, the *restriction* of "politics" was introduced into the June resolution by the deletion of the words "not for a moment" (forget the aim of overthrowing the autocracy) as well as by the addition of the words "the economic struggle is the *most widely* applicable means of drawing the masses into active political struggle. It is quite understandable that after such amendments had been introduced all the speakers on our side should one after another refuse to take the floor on the ground that further negotiations with people who were again turning towards Economism and who were striving to secure for themselves freedom of vacillation were useless.

"It was precisely the fact that the 'League' regarded the preservation of the independent features and the autonomy of *Rabocheye Dyelo* as the *sine qua non* of the durability of our future agreement, that *Iskra* regarded as the rock upon which our agreement fell to pieces" [*Two Congresses*, p. 25]. This is very inexact. We never had any designs against *Rabocheye Dyelo's* autonomy.* We did indeed *absolutely refuse to recognise* the independence of its features, if by "independent features" is meant independence on questions of principle regarding theory and practice: The June resolutions did indeed absolutely repudiate *such* independence of features because, in practice, such "independent features" meant, as we have said already, vacillation and support for the vacillations that now prevail among us, and the intolerable confusion that reigns in party affairs. *Rabocheye Dyelo's* articles in its issue No. 10, and its "amendments" clearly revealed its desire to preserve precisely this kind of independence of features, and such a desire naturally and inevitably led to a rupture and a declaration of war. But we were all ready to recognise *Rabocheye Dyelo's* "independent features" in the sense that it should concentrate on definite literary functions. A

---

* That is if the editorial consultations that were proposed in connection with the establishment of a joint supreme council of the combined organisations are not to be regarded as a restriction of autonomy. But in June *Rabocheye Dyelo* agreed to this.

proper distribution of functions naturally called for: (1) A scientific magazine, (2) a political newspaper, and (3) a popular symposium of articles and popular pamphlets. Only by agreeing to such a distribution of functions would *Rabocheye Dyelo* have proved that it *sincerely* desired to abandon once and for all its erring ways against which the June resolutions were directed. Only such a distribution of functions would have removed all possibility of friction and would have guaranteed a durable agreement which would at the same time have served as a basis for a fresh revival and new successes of our movement.

Not a single Russian Social-Democrat can have any doubts now about the fact that the final rupture between the revolutionary and opportunist tendencies was brought about, not by any "organisational" circumstances, but by the desire of the opportunists to perpetuate the independent features of opportunism and to continue to cause confusion of mind by arguments like those advanced by the Krichevskys and Martynovs.

CORRECTION TO *WHAT IS TO BE DONE*

THE Group of Initiators, to whom I referred in the pamphlet *What Is To Be Done?*,* have asked me to make the following correction to my description of the part they played in the attempt to reconcile the Social-Democratic organisations abroad:

Of the three members of this group only one left the "League" at the end of 1900; the others left in 1901, only after they had become convinced that it was impossible to obtain the "League's" consent to a conference with the foreign organisations of *Iskra* and the Revolutionary Social-Democrat Organisation, which is what the Group of Initiators had proposed. First of all, the Managing Committee of the "League" rejected the proposal for a conference on the ground that the persons making up the Group of Initiators were not "competent" to act as mediators and for that reason it at that time expressed the desire to enter into direct contact with the *Iskra* organisation abroad. Soon after, however, the Managing Committee of the "League" informed the Group of Initiators that after the appearance of the first number of *Iskra* containing the report of the split in the "League," it had altered its decision and no longer desired to have communication with *Iskra*. After this, how can one explain the statement made by a member of the Managing Committee of the "League" that the "League's" rejection of a conference was called forth *entirely* by its dissatisfaction with the composition of the Group of Initiators? It is true that it is equally difficult to explain why the Managing Committee of the "League" agreed to a conference in June last; for the remarks contained in the first issue of *Iskra* still remained in force and *Iskra's* "hostility" to the "League" was still more strongly expressed in the first volume of *Zarya* and in No. 4 of *Iskra*, both of which appeared prior to the June conference.

Iskra, No. 18, April 1, 1902.

* See p. 169.—*Ed.*

THE END